I0160299

BECOMING THE BEST VERSION OF YOU

A GUIDE TO SELF-REALIZATION AND PERSONAL TRANSFORMATION

Dr. Christian A. Wetie

CHRISTIAN A. WETIE
Publisher
North Carolina, USA

Copyright © 2019
Becoming the Best Version of
You
By Dr. Christian A. Wetie

All rights reserved.
This book, or parts thereof, may
not be reproduced in any form
without permission.

CONTENTS

Contents 3

Preface ix

Introduction xix

PART 1: BECOMING THROUGH SELF-KNOWLEDGE 1

1   IDENTITY CLARITY 5
    Identity At Birth 6
    Self-Actualization: A Key To Unlock Your Potential 6
    Self-Realization: A Key To Unleash Your Best Self 9
    Understanding Satisfaction 11
        Satisfaction Vs. Pleasure 11
        Job Satisfaction 12
    Benefits Of Clear Self-Identity 14
        An Inclusive Concept. 14
        Self-Worth 15

2   FACING THE UNPREDICTABLE 19
    Crisis: Time Of Pressure 21
    Existential Crisis 22
    Societal Crisis 22
    Human Formation And Growth 23
        Biological Process 26
        Unhealthy Biological Process 27
        External Factors of Maturation 28
    Personal Life Crisis 29
        Ill Maturation 29
    Making Lemonade Out Of Lemons 30

3   GAINING INSIGHTS 37
    Insights From Self-Reflection 38
    Retroflecting on Important Events 39

Losing The Battle But Winning The War 40
    Recognizing The Situation 41
    Staying Calm. 41
    Defining The Outcome 42
    Staying Positive And Inspired 42
Changing The Dynamics 43
    Your Turn 44
Reframing Life's Events 45
    Example 45
    Your Turn 46
Finding Your North Pole In Time Of Crisis 48
    Personal Story. 48

PART 2: SELF-ACTUALIZATION AND SELF-REALIZATION 52

4   What Type Of Person Are You? 55
Professional Qualities 57
    Machiavellianism 57
    Personality Type 58
    Proactive Personality 59

5   What Do You Do Best? 63
A Clear Identity Is An Asset 64
    Succeeding In What You Do. 65
    Do Not Live To Work, But Work To Live 67

6   Who Am I? 71
The Big Five Personality Traits 71
Using Psychiatric Lens 73
Using Sociological Lens 75
Using Psychological Lens 76
Identity: Personal Or Social Factor? 77

PART 3: BECOMING THROUGH SELF-ACCEPTANCE 81

7   Mastering Self-Acceptance 85
Self-Acceptance: A Key Ingredient For Life Satisfaction
    86

Self-Acceptance: A Key Ingredient For Personal
     Transformation 87
Fostering Self-Acceptance 88
Overcoming Obstacles To Self-Acceptance 90
     Desirable Self-Values 90
     Positive Perfectionism 90
     Positive Narcissism 91
Tapping On Your Good Side 95
Practicing Self-Affection 97
Giving From a Place of Abundance 98

8   Living Unapologetically 103
Liberty and Freedom Are Yours 105
Liberty and Freedom Are Not the Same 108
     Protecting Your Liberty and Freedom 109
     Quest for True Knowledge 110
     Correcting False Humility 112
     True Humility 112
Unapologetic Figures 113
     Condoleezza Rice 114
     Muhammad Ali 114

9   Becoming Through Your Predispositions 119
Tapping in Your Predispositions 119
Finding Your Sense of Self Through Your Predisposition
     120
Using Your Predisposition to Succeed in Your Career
     122

PART 4: IDENTITY CLARITY IN A HOST COUNTRY 125

10   The Adventurer Personality 129
Spy's Feature 133
Tourist's Feature 134
     Negative Mindset 135
     Positive Mindset 137
Prisoner's Feature 139
Missionary's Feature 139
Facing Your Discomfort 142

11   Your American Dream 147
        Being Enthusiatic And Creative 148
        Your Heart And Brain Are Connected 149
        Facing Your Discomfort 150
                Adapting To New Social Norms. 151
                Drawing A Bigger Picture 152
                Becoming Through Social Networking 153
                Overcoming Conflicting Social Norms 153
                Using Your Personal Authority 155
                The Power Of Personal Integration 156

12   Tapping Into Your Cultural Heritage 158
        Mastering Your Identity 158
        Reflecting On Meaningful "Chapters" 160
        Classic French Poetry 162
                Lorsque L'enfant Paraît 163
                When The Child Appears 165

Acknowledgements 167

The First Book 168

The Author 169

Bibliography 170

Index 179

To
My uncle,
Soufouo Edouard
a.k.a Le Makombe;
Accountant,
Businessperson, and Family
person

My sweet aunt,
Christine Tchougna,

And

My loving grandmother,
Madeleine Yemdo.

PREFACE

NOT PHILOSOPHICAL, BUT THEOLOGICAL

NOWADAYS, QUESTIONS SUCH AS "WHO AM I?" CAN BE TAKEN FOR granted in everyday life. But questions of that nature did not come easily to Søren Aabye Kierkegaard, a man who lost five of his siblings at a young age and whose father, Martin Kierkegaard, believed that such tragedy was related to his own conduct toward God. Although influenced by that tragedy and his father's belief, he believed no one is accountable for someone's else actions, behaviors, and no one ought to bear someone's else burden. For him, everyone can freely take ownership of his or her life and each person's life story is different and unique. His deeply held view led him to call off his engagement to Regina Olsen, his fiancée, and devoted most of his life reading and writing on matters important to him, and humankind. Kierkegaard was a learnt theologian, but his writings were of philosophical nature, which gave him a stellar reputation among most classic philosophers.

As one of the people who first wrestled with existential matters, Kierkegaard also believed that people cannot suffer indefinitely from their own past misconducts. He believed that everyone deserves to have a meaningful, successful, and satisfied life, despite past experiences. For him, anyone can have a second chance in life, but he or she must desire that fresh beginning, exercise a free will, and take charge of the course of life, including life's most important matters. The main challenge, he argued is our willingness to remove the Self from the noise of life, including our conventional way of life, in order to become the best of what we are and who we can be. In other words, becoming aware of who you are and transforming your personal life involve freeing yourselves from the unnecessary weight and burden related to everyday life.

For several years over the course of my life I struggled like many people to shed some light on existential questions and to come back from setbacks in personal and professional life. Reflecting on existential questions and searching for solutions to overcome life's unpredictable events, as well as facing common challenges can be addressed through the concepts of self-actualization and self-realization. The first one calls on to tapping into our potential. The latter, self-realization, calls on becoming the best of selves.

Although the literature offers extensive knowledge regarding existential questions, its findings ought not to be taken for granted or absolute, but instead as a framework or guide for self-discovery, self-empowerment, and self-enlightenment.

WELL-BEING: AN ANTHROPOLOGICAL AND SOCIOLOGICAL MATTER

CHILDREN BORN TO THIS WORLD, REGARDLESS OF THE ERA, GO through similar experiences of human development and growth. They all face the same challenges and difficulties, while being beset by existential questions and the ability to meet socioeconomic expectations. But, when it comes to areas pertaining to adapting to a way of life, children ought to experience proper maturation, upbringing, and social development. However, human beings ought to be life-long learners in order to live a meaning, successful, and satisfied life.

The practice of passing on knowledge from one generation to the next is a vital mean of preserving cultural and social norms and protecting future generations, at the collective level. At the personal level, the transfer of knowledge facilitates self-actualization and self-realization.

In past societies and in today's social environments, knowledge transfer from head-of-households to children is not only an important aspect of nurturing a child, but it is also a vital element in forming and grooming a child's sense of self. For example, in the United States, the adult–youth transfer of knowledge toward development and growth is facilitated in the community by school officials, counselors or therapists, mentors, extended family members, and religious leaders.

In general, parents' level of care, folk knowledge, formal education, and one's own life experience are main factors that shape children's upbringing, including their wellbeing, for soon they would become adolescents and young adults. If in past society, raising a child was a community matter, in modern and postmodern societies, it has increasingly become an individual matter. Such social shift comes with significant implications, at the individual, communal, and societal levels.

Interestingly, research in anthropology and sociology indicates that inappropriate upbringing of a child—at the individual and societal levels—has short-term and long-term implications especially among children, teenagers, and young adults. Let's keep in mind that adult crime is also another implication of an ill-development. Moreover, children who come to this world face similar challenges and difficulties, but those who came into an environment which has gone through numerous socioeconomic changes and transformation, natural and man-made disasters; racial and gender discrimination; and financial and economic depressions are susceptible to face more difficult challenges and conditions than those who do not. For example, some of those children who are born into more complex and poorly integrated socioeconomic environment do even face greater challenges when parents lack proper education, folk knowledge; are financially unprepared; and are stuck in some sort of addiction and inadequate social safety net.

In recent years, mental health experts and social activists have taken to the mainstream the high rate of mentally challenged people and the high rate of incarceration to highlight the situation of millions of people. For example, the U.S. population is 5% of the world population but registers 25% of incarceration at the global level. That means, at the national level, 716 people for every hundred thousand residents are incarcerated.

The high rate of incarceration is an evidence of a socioeconomic system that needs improvement and the long-term consequences of inadequate personal development and growth. Furthermore, the challenges and adversities that people may experience in various stages of human growth can be seen in institutions, such as psychiatric hospitals, mental rehabilitation centers, foster homes, centers for drugs addiction, as well as community centers geared toward social reinsertion and empowering victims of domestic violence and abuse. Therefore, fostering self-knowledge as it relates to existential question is an immediate and long-term approach to facilitate self-actualization and self-realization, among people and communities of various economic classes and social background.

To conclude, research findings reveal that people who experience inappropriate human growth are likely to experience episodes of crisis. Consequently, it might be beneficial for some people not to blame themselves for their predicaments. They should be open to new ideas and fresh perspectives in the face of life's unpredictable challenges and obstacles.

TAKING ON THE CHALLENGE

WHO YOU CAN BECOME AND WHAT YOU CAN DO CANNOT BE achieved through a single event or sporadic effort. But it requires a significant level of persistence and perseverance to see it become a reality. One way to stay the course is to break down the dynamics at play into two elements: Factors and variables. Next, you take a close look at each of them, in order to have a proper understanding of be in control of the experience.   Factors are forces that greatly determine who and or what you can become. Some of those forces are external and others are internal. Whether there are external or internal, sometimes there is something you can do about those forces and sometimes there is nothing you can do about them. Moreover, variables are things you could use to face those forces. For example, let us consider an unpredictable event in our life as a factor that hinders to achieve a goal. Therefore, that event can break us, but it might also make us stronger in life. A closer look at the event or factor can help us to see what it made off, which can be referred as variables. Based on that analysis you can not only be in control of the whole dynamic at play, but you can also formulate a proper plan of action to achieve your goal. The challenge in transforming your life lies not only in your level of self-actualization and self-realization, but also in your willingness to adapt to your environment and forge your own identity.

Failing to adapt to life's major changes can get you stuck, frustrated, unhappy, dissatisfied, and unable to unlock your potential, including becoming your best self. Solutions to obstacles are often within reach. To illustrate that, real life stories of several well-known people are used in this book.

Now, let us be candid. Have you ever heard statement like: "He/she has no life," "he/she is still acting like a kid," or "he/she needs to grow up." "The world in which we live sets norms and expectations. Some are objectives. Others are subjective. Those norms come in various types; some are natural while others are man-made. Natural norms are, for instance, the stages of human development: childhood, adolescence, and adulthood or old age. In each of those stages, people have expectations, such as expecting a 3-year-old child to walk or a 12-year-old child to take a bath and get dress— without parental help, in either scenario.

The development and transformation of our physical body are not isolated from our intellectual, emotional, and psychological aptitude, as we go through stages of human development; therefore, it is essential that we go through a healthy process of growth during maturation. However, in the situation of biological complication, there can be adverse consequences in some areas of human development and growth, from childhood to adulthood. To be more specific, each stage of maturation is tied to our health, including our intellectual, emotional, and psychological abilities. Therefore, while normal growth yields desirable results, abnormal growth has adverse consequences on our emotional and learning aptitude. For example, abnormal process can impede a child ability to read, write, and comprehend basic social concepts. Furthermore, it is important to highlight that abnormal development in one stage can potentially affect the next stage and, ultimately impede the ability to live a rewarding, meaningful, and satisfied life.

PURPOSE

JUVENILE DELINQUENCY MENTAL HEALTH ILLNESS, ADULT'S CRIME AND other pathological issues, and deliberate unethical behavior in the workplace and in the community underline real-world challenges and problems people need to overcome in order to live up to their socioeconomic expectations, and most importantly to achieve their personal goals and see their aspirations become a reality. Moreover, people from all walks of life ought to overcome those social phenomena, as they strive to live their best life and become their best selves. However, it is important to recognize that most socioeconomic problems and phenomena are potential ingredients of revolt to an unjust system (political and socioeconomic) that fail to meet the need of a significant number of people. In other words, people may not necessarily revolt to a system; but instead, they thirst for growth and success in complex society regulated by unjust system, in favorable environment.

Much has been done to correct and meet people's needs at the community and personal levels. Some of the solutions include:

- Employment creation
- Education and formal training
- Recreational infrastructure
- Entrepreneurship
- Lifelong learning

This book is a guide for self-actualization and self-realization through self-knowledge and self-enlightenment, based on proven concepts, principles and life stories of well-known figures from various walks of life in Sports, Entertainment, and Politics. This book was carefully written to encourage and inspire its readers to thrive for a meaningful and successful life at the personal and professional levels.

"Becoming the Best Version of You" is a useful guide to people interested in wellness and wellbeing. It offers abstract and concrete elements to help you stretch your self-knowledge, redefine or hone sense of self; and actualize and maximize your potential, where it seems appropriate.

This book is not only a valuable read for personal and professional needs, but it is also valuable additional reading material in colleges and universities.

AN EXAMPLE OF BECOMING THE BEST VERSION

If there is someone whose life best exemplifies how to become the best version of self is the 44th President of the United States, Barack Obama. He is someone who has been able to use life's circumstances to forge a strong and rich personal identity and create a bright future for himself and millions of people in the United States and around the world. It is no secret for anyone that he barely knew his father, who had come to the United States from Kenya, Africa, for academic reasons. He divorced Barack's mother, a white woman from Kansas, and returned to his homeland. Raised in a middle-class family, between his mother and grandparents, Barack Obama had a trouble life due to the social status and his mixed ethnicity. The former U.S President, Barack Obama had also acknowledged that he used to smoke dope and drink to shield from life's obstacles and challenges. But later in life, he decided to face his reality, develop his identity, and change the course of his life. As a result of that, as a presidential candidate of the United States, he tapped on the same factors and elements, such as being raised by a single mother and being of mixed ethnicity.   The rest is history.

INTRODUCTION

PACE OF LIFE

IN THE UNITED STATES, MANY POLITICAL FIGURES CLAIM THAT AMERICA IS A "Beacon of Hope" and the "Land of opportunity for all." Similarly, around the globe, the United States is perceived as such. In fact, an aspect of the American dream is the pursuit of happiness. Although that ideal is highly celebrated, life in the United States, along with the dynamics of its socioeconomic environment, is in many levels challenging, difficult, and hectic. One of the primary reasons is that most of the U.S. population is deeply engaged in the pursuit of money, power, and fame. Popular beliefs include achievements, freedom, and free enterprises. It must be for these reasons that the words of Francis Scott are included in the U.S. national anthem, the Star-Spangled Banner: America is the home of the brave."

In most U.S. cities, people walk, speak, and eat fast. You can say living in these cities is like "life in the fast lane." Time is of essence. The fast pace of life is constantly increasing, while the environment is constantly changing. People must adapt to the pace of life and the environment. Some people would tell say, "You swim or sink." Other people would recommend you to "Shoot for the stars and if you happen to miss, you will still land at the top."

Most of the U.S. working population, including migrants, is "overworked," many people can become "busy bodies," and everything seems to be endless. The constraint of life, along with the U.S. job market, is a major cause of a lifestyle of "paycheck to paycheck" among millions of people. In fact, according to a recent survey, nearly two-thirds of the U.S. population lacks enough savings to cover $400 unexpected expenses, such as vehicle repair or home appliance purchase. For some people, it is not about money; however, unfortunately they are only likely to find meaning and sense of self when working, which makes them workaholic. Living to work comes with adverse consequences. U.S Born and immigrants alike see their physical and mental health well-being deteriorate. In general, people in America struggle to live a rewarding, meaningful, and fulfilled life.

For the majority of the U.S. population, the idea of the American dream is about achieving financial stability, pursuit of happiness, fame, and influence. In recent years, it also means freedom of speech, identity choices, and social equality. However, U.S. born residents and non-U.S. born residents, including residents, experience dissimilar challenges and life predicaments.

U.S. BORN

The American dream is achieved through personal goal achievement and free enterprise. However, for anyone, achieving the American dream can simply become an illusion, a dream that may never become a reality, despite overcoming typical challenges among U.S. born citizens. Challenges may include working long hours, studying sleepless nights, training or practicing hard, and, for some, overcoming racial prejudice and discrimination.

For the majority of U.S. born citizens, the main challenge in turning their daydream into a reality involves making sense of who they are, as a person and as a human being, in a knowledge-based and complex socioeconomic environment.

NON-U.S. BORN

For the millions of people who have migrated to the United States, achieving their American dream is not given due to typical human migration challenges, such as language barrier, learning unfamiliar social norms or proper behavior, constant feeling of homesickness, and being *victimized* during economic decline. For many immigrants in the Land of the Free and Home of the Brave, achieving an American dream includes a progressive integration in a socioeconomic environment influenced by illusionism. Therefore, millions of non-U.S. born citizens face the risk of drifting away from their true self, needs, and higher purpose, and ultimately missing the opportunity of realizing who they are, as a person and as a human being.

Underestimating the benefits of developing a strong and rich identity comes with adverse consequences such as pathological behaviors, and psychological and mental unbalanced, as witness in either group of the U.S population. For example, recent statistics suggests the U.S hold 25% of the world's prisoners. While U.S. born citizens face the likelihood to be in a condition of abuse of illegal drugs, mental illness, and incarceration, immigrants struggle to integrate in their host country. In short, in one hand, U.S. born citizens are primarily concerned with financial freedom and life satisfaction. On the other hand, immigrants are primarily concerned making America their home country.

Regardless of the natural birthplace of each member of the U.S. population, almost everyone is generally concerned with living successful and happy life.

For each group of the population, an alternative solution for overcoming everyday challenges and obstacles is to become the best version of self, which require developing a strong and rich identity, especially in an individualistic society, which celebrates personal freedom expression and free-enterprise.

LASTING HAPPINESS IS WITHIN

ANY PEOPLE WOULD GO INTO GREAT LENGTHS TO BE ADMIRED, praised, and even loved by altering their physical appearance. Every year in the United States, $12 billion are spent in surgical procedures for physical enhancement. It is said that you only get one chance to create a lasting impression. However, caring for your body and physical appearance is not only to make that first impression; to feel happy and comfortable under your own skin also requires inner well-being. But if you only focus on physical appearance, you might not experience lasting joy and growth from within. When you overlook your inner well-being the life that you have. It is vital that we do not fall prey of what big companies seek to sell to us through ads. Your physical appearance represents only one percent of who you are.

In addition to caring for your external appearance, you can also address your inner needs and aspirations to achieve a balanced and harmonious growth in almost all aspects of your life (personal, professional, intimate relationships with close and extended families).

One effective and successful approach to achieve harmony in your life is to firmly take the path of growth inside out. A clear identity helps you to shed light on who you are, as a person, what type of person you are, and what you can do, including work-related activities that you enjoy the most. A strong and rich identity does not negate healthy and attractive physical appearance; on the contrary, it includes accepting your physical features, an essential aspect of life happiness.

PART 1

BECOMING THROUGH SELF-KNOWLEDGE

The tragedy of life is not death but what we let die inside of us while we live.

—Norman Cousins

In the social jungle of human existence, there is no feeling of being alive without a sense of identity.

—Erik Erikson

1

IDENTITY CLARITY

A CLEAR SELF-IDENTITY IS A KEY INGREDIENT TOWARD TRANSFORMING YOUR life and becoming the best version of who you were made to be. A clear identity starts in childhood to adulthood. Your identity is an important ingredient of your predisposition, preferences, and styles. It is a key element of your sense of self. Without having a clear identity, people are susceptible to wander in life, to feel disoriented and unable to face challenges likely to transform their lives, including becoming the best version of them. You can think of clear identity as a crucial element to know who you are and what kind of life you want to have. In other words, developing a clear identity requires self-awareness, which consequently yields into high level of self-actualization and self-realization. It is important to note that the concept of self-identity, though subjective is more objective than subjective, as compared to other self-concepts, such as self-esteem, and self-image. In this chapter, you will learn how to become the best version of you through self-actualization and self-realization. This chapter explains how you acquire your identity and how you could strengthen it to become the best version of who you are.

IDENTITY AT BIRTH

A N INFANT IS PRONE TO INHERIT PARENTS' BIOLOGICAL TRAITS SUCH AS muscle composition and temperament, which explains why at birth, and during infancy, parents' physical features are already noticeable on a child. Even some of the parents' non-physical features, such as personality, begin to emerge outwardly in the early life years of a child. Therefore, it is appropriate to say that some personality traits are inherited, not chosen. But in those early years, a child can still show unique qualities, not related to those of the biological parents. The time period and the environment in which a child is born should not also be underestimated. Traits are bound to time and space. In forming personal identity, one of the main challenges over the course of life is defining one's sense of self. It can be challenging because the self is a mix of the parents' identity and the world surrounding the child. Therefore, from the premise that, at birth, people have no other identity aside from being humans, one can assert that people are not born with absolute identities.

SELF-ACTUALIZATION: A KEY TO UNLEASH YOUR POTENTIAL

M ASLOW'S THEORY REVEALS THAT PEOPLE ARE BEINGS DRIVEN AND influenced by physiological needs, which are grouped in two categories: *Lower-order* needs such as nutrition, shelter, and safety, in one hand. Higher order needs such achievement, prestige, and recognition, in other hand. Once our lower-order needs are met, we thrive for higher-order, which are crucial ingredients to becoming the best version of us.

Our sense of self is tied to our desires and needs. Once we no longer worry about our lower-order needs such as food, shelter, clothes, and protection, we become internally driven by *higher-order* needs such as esteem (respect, admiration, or autonomy) and other social factors (affection, acceptance, or relationship). With higher order needs we can possibly be intrinsically driven and motivated; we can maintain a high energy level, as well as attain a stable state of growth, fulfillment, and happiness. Higher-order needs are precursors to self-actualization, which is about maximizing on potential. Like some experts' viewpoint on performance, I share the belief that self-actualization is about tapping on areas of strengths, as opposed to attempting to focusing on areas of weakness. Achieving self-actualization is not given but earned through the longing to meet our high-order needs, such as self-respect, self-admiration, and independence. Therefore, developing a clear understanding of your identity is an essential factor in identifying realistic and suitable higher needs. Maslow, the father of theory of needs underscores that people drive toward self-actualization greatly influences their personalities.

The basis of self-actualization is an effective approach to becoming your ideal self and living the life you hope for. The benefit of using self-actualization is that achieving primarily depend on your will and desire, as opposed to criteria such as how much money you make, how many friends you have, or where you come from.

In your journey of self-actualization, you can make sense of your life, because you would have the opportunity to assess your achievements, examine your self-worth, as well as any room of growth. In that journey you will be more confident about maximizing your potentials. As a result of it, you can take the necessary actions and adopt the necessary behavior to redefine your life. Ways to enrich and enjoy your self-actualization experience include sharing your personal story with people and connect with them in nonjudgement manner toward yourself.

We live in a fast and dynamic environment, in which we ought to strive and thrive; however, we could limit ourselves without proper self-knowledge, particularly about who we are, as a person and as a human being. A clear self-identity allows you to affirm your personality's traits, skills, preferences, and styles. Your self-identity is as an invisible bank account available to you to the extent that you are willing to understand it and act on it. Further you understand who you are as human being, and a person stronger you will get, farther you will go and higher you will climb, and experience greater satisfaction in life. With a strong and rich identity you can expect to thrive and seize opportunities; sustain momentum; face and overcome challenges and difficulties; transcend beliefs and ways of life that are obsolete; see through ambiguity; and go beyond expectations. Self-actualization is as a secret pathway to transforming your life and becoming the best version of you.

Self-actualization can be achieved by collecting information and placing them into proper context. It includes looking at facts, being nonjudgmental toward self. For example, Annie is a young lady, a single parent of an 8-year-old boy. She was struggling to make end meet. She decided to do something about it by taking advantage of her areas of strengths. She started to educate herself on personal finances and financial independence. She sought help from experts and friends. She examined what she could do to improve her life and with of her son. In short, she actualized her skills, competencies, and general knowledge. But first, she looked for facts and faces her difficulties. She worked on becoming the best version of her, each day at a time.

Self-actualization is about considering and uncovering fresh and unorthodox perspectives to matters that are important to your welfare. When achieved, you can expect to feel rejuvenated mentally, emotionally, and psychologically. Lived experiences strengthened our lives. What we need the most to develop our identity is a desire to grow and become our best self. Self-actualization is about our ability to meet your higher-order needs. The level of self-actualization you can attain in this lifetime is primarily tied to uncovering your intrinsic and extrinsic needs, in other words, you need to be aware of you are and what you have in order to become the person you were meant to be.

SELF-REALIZATION: A KEY TO UNLEASH YOUR BEST SELF

SELF-REALIZATION CAN BE DESCRIBED AS THE AWAKENING OF THE SOUL AND human spirit. In other words, to achieve self-realization ones need to be awaken, at least, mentally, emotionally, and psychologically. Although at the practical level, individual achievement is generally tied to our skills and abilities, at the abstract level; individual achievement primarily lies on the degree to which our soul and human spirit are enlightened. Self-realization ought not to be optional or imposed, but holistically and organically driven by a genuine desire and belief in betterment for oneself, the community, and the world around.

In addition to self-actualization, self-realization is key to transform your life because it allows you take stock of your potential and align it with who you are, including your values, beliefs, and what matter most for you. Note that when you become more interested in getting to know who you are as a person and as a human being, you will be increasingly inclined to care about yourself as a whole, including your self-worth, which is an essential aspect to live a satisfying life. Furthermore, self-realization is also about becoming aware and attune with the world around. In other words, a strong and rich sense of self is a precursor to a well-enlightened self-realization.

Self-actualization and self-realization go together. A blurred soul and spirit can get you feel lost, undecided, stuck, and unable to navigate the complexity of everyday life. The famous fictional story of Alice and the Cat, by Lewis Carroll, illustrates best the need of clear direction in becoming your to becoming your best self.

In that fairy tale, Alice asked the cat, "Would you tell me, please, which way I ought to go from here?"

"That depends a good deal on where you want to get to," He replied.

"I don't much care where," Alice said.

"Then it doesn't matter which way you go," the Cat replied.

"So long as I get SOMEWHERE," Alice added, as an explanation.

"Oh, you're sure to do that ... if you only walk long enough," the Cat added.

In an ever-changing socio-economic environment, it is vital to be aware of who you are and what are at stake can be sometimes unclear and challenging. For that reason, it is essential to choose path that aligned with who are and what can help you to become your best self. When we do not know who we are, we are likely to depend on people for approval, instructions and advice. No one can best realize who you are and what is important to you, but you.

UNDERSTANDING SATISFACTION

SATISFACTION CAN BE DEFINED AS A STABLE STATE OF HAPPINESS AFTER addressing a specific challenge or obstacle. To be satisfied is to know who you are and what you want out any predicament you find yourself in and aiming to get a desirable outcome. Satisfaction comes from within. Many people would be happier in life, if they got a better understanding about how satisfaction can be attained. In this section, we will use job satisfaction to shed light on the concept of satisfaction, in general. Work is a basic and important aspect of our life. Everyone can relate with the idea of job satisfaction. In fact, research findings consistently suggest that 50% of people are usually unhappy with their job. For the common person, his or her level of satisfaction is not only tied to his or her job title, but also to his personal sense of self. Equally, people can perform well at work when they have a clear sense of self. Before taking a close look at the concept of job satisfaction, let us contrast satisfaction and pleasure in the next paragraph.

SATISFACTION VS. PLEASURE. While pleasure is described as a momentary happiness; satisfaction is described as creating a fortunate outcome or the ability to meet the requirement. Based on those descriptions, we can identify several features: Length of time, internal and external factors.

In the day-to-day life, when we experience a brief state of pleasure about something, we show that we are happy. Pleasure is a momentary, pleasant state of being. It is also an internal factor because we can choose to be happy. We can be happy for no apparent reason. That makes happiness an internal factor.

You can be satisfied after completing a challenging task at work or a school project. Satisfaction offers a permanent state of ease. The feeling you get from being satisfied is relatively a longer period, as compared to the pleasure you get from being happy. Next, the satisfaction you experience by completing your project, assignment, or goal is a state that you created. Therefore, satisfaction involves an internal and external factor. The internal factor in this scenario would be your energy and time. The external factor in this scenario would be the completion of the project.

In other words, happiness offers a momentary state of ease, while satisfaction offers permanent state of ease. Although we can easily of pleasure, experiencing a state of satisfaction can be difficult and challenging, but more rewarding and fulfilling than momentary happiness.

When you develop a clear self-identity, you are likely to be in state of permanence state of ease. In contrary, a superficial understanding of who you are can temporary satisfied, stuck, and unable to live a fulfilling life.

JOB SATISFACTION. Next, let us use the idea of job satisfaction to show the need to develop a strong and rich personal identity. Let us note that high job satisfaction does not equate with higher performance. Still, job satisfaction is an essential prerequisite to achieve and sustain long-term growth at the organizational and individual levels.

A report from the Society of Human Resource Management (SHRM) shows that 88% of employees were satisfied with their job, in 2015. From the premise that we spend about a third of our daily life at work and about a third of it in the bedroom. Consequently, job satisfaction and life satisfaction emerge as important aspects for a successful and happy life.

Increasing job satisfaction requires better pay, work activity, and personal achievement. Although workers become happy and motivated with better pay, higher earning does not necessarily mean job satisfaction. Work activity and personal fulfillment are also essential ingredients. The compensation plan alone does not ensure job satisfaction. Much of it has been learned in the selling sector. For example, sales organizations constantly offer monetary rewards to drive motivation. But research indicates that many organizations still industry registers high rates of turnover and job burnout. Thus, high earning does not make satisfied workers.

Enough evidence suggests that high productivity and satisfied workers require the right people in the right environment. To be more specific, at the organizational level, job satisfaction is a combination of several factors that include a positive relationship, acceptable working conditions, and sound policies. At the individual level, achieving job satisfaction requires being aware of individual qualities, strengths, weaknesses, and areas for improvement. Consequently, unless you clearly understand who you are, what you can do, and who you can be, it can be difficult for you to be satisfied. Taking a close look at the concept of self-identity might be helpful to develop a strong and rich understanding of who you are, at the personal and professional levels.

BENEFITS OF CLEAR SELF-IDENTITY

N LESS THAN 60 SECONDS, OVER SIX MILLION RESULTS CAME UP FROM A Google search about self-esteem. In that search, the popular image of a cat seeing itself as a lion or a big cat on the mirror also came up. Evidently, millions of people around the globe concern themselves with the topic of self-esteem. One of the shortcomings of the concept of self-esteem is the emphasis on feelings, which for many people come in form of emotional rollercoaster.

You can enhance your self-perception without relying on how people around you think of you. The theory of self-identity offers the opportunity to look at ourselves within a social context. In other words, with self-identity you can focus on recognizing your qualities and abilities, as they relate to the environment in which you live, work, and play.

AN INCLUSIVE CONCEPT. Self-identity is an inclusive self-concept identity in comparison to other self-concepts such self-image or self-esteem. For example, self-esteem places an emphasis on our feelings. However, with the theory of self-identity, we can emphasize on self-knowledge, as opposed to temporary feelings. Self-identity goes beyond the intellectual aspect of our life. With self-identity, we can address your cognitive and emotional needs. With the concept of self-esteem, just as self-image, we can address our emotional and psychological needs. The popular picture of the cat seeing itself as a lion best illustrates how the concept of self-image can be helpful to us in identifying our *ideal self*. Self-Identity helps you to recognize your *actual self* and your ideal self. Although self-concept is a subjective way of self-assessment in general—compared to self-image and self-esteem—self-identity is not only an inclusive concept, but it also tends to be more objective.

SELF-WORTH. A clear understanding of your personal identity can enhance your self-worth. The amount of money you can earn is largely tied to your self-view. Consequently, if you have a clear knowledge about yourself, you can earn more than otherwise.

Setting goals and directing resources toward achieving them are common practices for people. Similarly, when you have a good understanding of yourself, you can identify the right goals and make the right decision to allocate your resources toward achieving them.

Sometimes, we set goals just because they are attractive or because we want to please someone else. When we achieve those goals, we are still not truly satisfied, though we just accomplished something challenging and commendable, but we still experience a feeling of emptiness.

A good understanding about yourself can be helpful to accurately allocate your time, energy, and money. In addition, you are likely to be intrinsically driven toward achieving those goals. Simply put, not all goals are equal. Some offer momentary pleasure. Others offer lasting gratifications. Knowing yourself a little better will spare you from unnecessary frustration and disappointment, as you make the right decision on important life matters.

In addition, earning the income you want is not only about having the proper skills and abilities related to a profession. It is also about your attitude, expectations of the environment in which you live, and your general knowledge about your profession or line of work. Those aspects require having a clear self-identity, because that it allows you to not only tap on the potential needed to hold the position, but also to assert the appropriate qualities and features related to the position. In terms of self-worth, part of your ability to earn a desired income level is also related to your core belief and emotional energy level. Therefore, emphasizing on tasks, skills, and abilities alone can be limiting and ineffective.

Common questions such as "How much do you want?" or "How much do you crave?" are attempts to challenge or stretch the emotional and psychological belief system. The likelihood to meet a desire or aspiration is usually tied to important determinants of your success: how much you know about the matter at hand and how much you know about yourself. But, a rich understanding of your self-identity can boost self-confidence and consequently the ability to boost a level of income. It is important to note that, earning less than what you believe is your worth does not mean you cannot have a position under your credential, including work experience. Some events in your life may force you to take a job below your qualifications. Still, you have a good understanding of your self-worth and are willing to take a low-paying job so that you can weather storms in your life.

Finally, a good understanding of who you are can be valuable for you to identify and invest your time and interest on activities in which you need or want to be involved. Your hobbies, for example, are important aspects of your well-being; therefore, being aware of what type of activities that make you happy can help to attain a stage of self-realization.

To conclude, the concept of self-identity is based on recognizing your abilities, as they fit in the environment where you live and work. By using the concept, you can help improve the quality of your life and enhance your lifestyle.

It always seems impossible until it's done.

—Nelson Mandela

I am no bird; and no net ensnares me: I am a free human being with an independent will.

—Charlotte Brontë, *Jane Eyre*

2

FACING THE UNPREDICTABLE

LIFE IS COMPLEX. AN ATTEMPT TO UNDERSTAND IT AS A STRAIGHT A LINE without landmines may be naïve, frustrating or disappointing. Life is not only is a complex phenomenon, but people are also complex beings. Consequently, challenges, obstacles, and problems we face are undoubtedly multifaceted. But fortunately, solutions to predicaments we face are within reach. Mary E. Copeland and Meghan Markle's life stories are two of countless examples that illustrate solutions to even unpredictable events in our life are within own hands.

Copeland's life story illustrates best how anyone in search of a solution can get satisfactory results, despite disparaging conduct from people with formal training. Copeland, now an author, educator, and advocate of mental health, was once told by a trained professional that no information was available to help her recover from her mental challenges. Another trained professional indicated to her the cause of her inability to function well was only "a fiction." After spending many years in psychiatric hospitals, she had decided to take the matter into her own hands. She had ultimately regained control over her mental problems. Now, she can unapologetically claim that she has been able to fulfill her aspirations. Copeland is a well-established professional at the national and international levels.

Today, the idea of mental crisis makes many of us uncomfortable and becomes a stigma. Crisis is a human experience, sometimes unavoidable. Until we recognize it as such, it can be more difficult to face chaotic situations, make and transcend crisis' related moments in life. most importantly, we will also be able to learn from it, and use it as steppingstone for the best future. Several life events might cause us to go through a crisis. Whatever the reasons are, common life crises are at times no fault of our own. In the next paragraphs, we can take a close look at existential and human development crisis, including societal and individual causes of crises.

Meghan Markle, former film actress, now Duchess of Sussex in U.K, has also experienced periods of personal crisis. She struggled to find her own sense identity, not only because she's a multiracial identity, but also because some people around did not help accept who she is as a mixed-race person, which made it difficult for her to know who she was and affirm what she can do.

When she was still a girl, she said to her father, a Caucasian, "my teacher told me to check the box for Caucasian." She explained that she could not do that and left the box blank "...an absolute incomplete-much like how I felt." Over the course of her professional career as well she experienced period of identity, primary because people did not know where she would fit Hispanic, Italian, or African American, but never Caucasian, by birth right. A major factor of her successful career and life is tied to her decision to embrace her diversity and stand for what she believes to be.

CRISIS: TIME OF PRESSURE

C RISIS CAN BE DESCRIBED AS A MAJOR THAT HAS DISRUPTED A day-to-day life. Crisis is a natural phenomenon. Sometimes they can cause major interruptions in people's ways of life. But it is part of life. People go through period of crisis because they feel threaten by a specific situation. A situation of discrepancy between an ideal situation and what they experience. Stress, for example, is a common issue that causes discrepancy in our self-interest and well-being. A stressful situation can be described as the amount of pressure exerted in our intellectual, emotional, and psychological aptitude. It is the inability, at least in one of those areas, to appropriately handle or adapt to a specific level of pressure or situation. Stress begins in our brain and manifests itself through our nervous system and can be felt in various parts of our biological system.

Typically, when we go through a phase of crisis, you can become anxious because of unknown outcomes related to an event or situation; our thought processes become disorganized and our ability to think clearly diminishes. Crisis disrupts your personal order or way of life, including your biopsychosocial balance. You can say that crisis makes you lose your mental, emotional, and psychological sanity. In other words, your sense of self (i.e., your knowledge of your personal identity, including your skills and abilities) as it relates to the environment in which you live and work, might decline, due to a dramatic event. The level to which your sense of self is directly associated to the severity of the lived

EXISTENTIAL CRISIS

IT IS BEYOND DEBATE THAT EACH PERSON IS UNIQUELY DIFFERENT FROM THE REST of his or her fellow human being, although there are degrees of similarity with others. Existential questions are about lived events and therefore ought to be addressed at a personal level. Facing existential questions might have been *challenging* for some people, *somewhat difficult* for some people, and *difficult* for others. However, research literature about existentialism shows that facing existential questions usually yields identity crisis. Although scholars across disciplines and fields of study have concerned themselves with those questions and the like, each of us, regardless of our walk of life, still face them. Despite the rich repository of knowledge related to those them. Many of us seem to have more questions than answers. Answers to existential questions are personal lived experiences. A popular suggestion on handling existential crisis is avoiding making it personal, but instead a shared experience among people of various walks of life.

SOCIETAL CRISIS

F ROM A BROAD STANDPOINT, EXISTENTIAL CRISIS CAN BE RELATED TO SOME variables at the societal level. For example, when someone finds it difficult to get a career match due to ethnicity, a life partner due to financial and economic reasons, or an opportunity to interact with other members of the community in which he lives, based on sexual orientation; or feels insecure about wear a type of cloth, driving or walking in some residential communities, or being of specific gender group, such person may experience an identity crisis.

Markle's letter to Procter & Gamble, prompted by the company's TV ad illustrate best individual consequences of societal norms. In the middle school, Markle and her peers were asked to analyze several advertisement contents, one of them Ivory dishwasher soap by Proctor and Gamble. The young girl strongly felt the advertisement line "Women all over America are fighting greasy pots and pans" did not reflect her parents' everyday life and values, certainly, including hers. Her sense of identity and personal belief prompted her to write a letter to the company, who did not, discarded her views, but revamped the advertisement's message - content.

At the individual level, identity is also tied to the natural process of human of growth: childhood, adolescence, and adulthood. In other words, someone's identity clarity is tied to how he goes through each stage of human growth. Conversely, experiencing ill maturation can yield into identity crisis. Maladaptive maturation can be described as an abnormal process of human development. Peer pressure, for example, is among factors that impede a normal process of maturation, specifically among teenagers and young adults. Signs of identity crisis include dropping out of school, stubbornness, imprudence, and the inability to decide which academic major to pursue.

HUMAN FORMATION AND GROWTH

H UMAN BEINGS DEVELOP THROUGH SYSTEMATIC EVENTS OF PRUNING excitatory neurons, crucial for adapting to the environment and life conditions. To further our understanding of human's life crisis, it can be useful to briefly describe the concept of maturation. Human maturation is a dynamic process of *pruning*, including *neuronal stimulation*. It is a process of human development. Although maturation different from maturity, the process of maturation has a direct effect on people's state of maturity.

BIOLOGICAL PROCESS. One way to evaluate someone's degree of maturation is to assess his or her ability to adapt to the environment in which he lives, works, and plays. For instance, a child's relentless desire to walk shows best his effort and enthusiasm about the environment, in which he must adapt to strive, thrive, and gain personal status. It is evident that the child's level of stimulation is in part not only tied to how he views himself or how he wants to accomplish his aspirations and goals, but also how he carries himself.

In other words, a child's process of maturation has not only a direct implication on the extent to that child is stimulated about the world, but also his or he level of maturity about matters important in life. The process of maturation has a significant effect on human development and growth, including well-being. It has an impact on people's whole being. Maturation, through pruning, begins at the embryonic stage.

You already know that maturation occurs through neuronal stimulation or nerve impulses. In this regard, experimental psychology researchers have concerned themselves with understanding the various stages of human development. Biological study shows that your heart is the first body parts formed at the embryonic stage; your brain is at the center of the process of maturation, which happens through neuronal activity. Study also shows the brain and the nervous system are essential in the process of maturation, which primarily occurs through systematic and continual pruning events of excitatory neurons. One of the benefits of pruning stage is to ensure that your brain develops and functions well as you go through phases of human formation, development, and growth.

Pruning is a progressive event of the neuron and one of the most important events happens at puberty. It is one of the most important development stages because, as you already know, puberty is a major phase in human bodily transformation and maturation, including brain development. A late maturation is due to delayed pruning occurrence and an early maturation is due to an early pruning event as well. Therefore, pruning must be correctly done, if not, there will be adverse consequences in the near or distant future.

INAPPROPRIATE BIOLOGICAL PROCESS. Some people might go through personal crisis due to no fault of their own and maturational crises illustrate best such scenario. To understand maturational crisis, let us briefly take a close look at how biological development happens, first. Study shows the process of pruning begins even before birth. The embryonic stage of human life includes an overproduction of ephemeral excitatory neurons, which undergo pruning process before birth and during infancy, puberty, and the early stage of human development. Maturational crises can be described as inappropriate pruning processes.

An early maturation can be described as reduced pruning of glutamate excitatory neurons. At puberty, for example, an important phase in human maturation and brain development, pruning events might not occur in a timely manner, which can have adverse consequences on a child's brain. Adolescents, who go through an early maturation process, are likely to have an increased neural excitability, which can cause a child to be prone to abnormal mood change, manic and depressive behavior with no apparent causes, for example.

On the contrary, late maturation is susceptible to yield into a reduced neuronal activity. Consequently, the person might later develop symptoms of schizophrenia, which explains why pharmacological treatments to related disorders include antidepressants, to lower the level of excitement.

EXTERNAL FACTORS OF MATURATION. The brain plays a critical role in human life. This is also true during the stages of development and growth, particularly at maturation phases. For example, at puberty, teenagers extensively pick on ideas and thoughts; they explore, examine, analyze, reflect, and ask questions about varying topics, at least several, if not numerous times. Such mental exercise helps a child or everyone for that matter to get an answer on any given concern, such as his personal identity. A child who gets honest and satisfying answers is likely to experience a healthy process of human development. However, if a child gets partial truth on basic and fundamental questions, such as who his biological parents are, or his own national identity then that child is susceptible to get confused about his personal identity.

Due to inappropriate pruning occurrence, some people might go through episodes of personal crisis, later in life. Crises related to inappropriate pruning events can also be understood as maturational crises.

PERSONAL LIFE CRISIS

CRISES CAN BE DESCRIBED AS LIFE'S EVENT THAT CAUSES US TO experience a nervous breakdown. Crises usually happen in early or late adulthood years. Mid-life crisis is a typical example of identity crisis. Some experts indicate that while mid-life crisis among female last longer, between two to five years, male mid-life crisis can last between three to ten years. This part of the book uses the concept of self-discrepancy to describe how people can experience personal crises.

Our identity is influenced by three domains: *Actual self*, *ideal self*, and *ought self*. The self includes characteristics you possess. Contrary to the actual self, the ideal self is who or what you desire to become. It is about the potentials you desire to develop. Lastly, ought self is about our sense of obligation. Its stresses on functions and roles we believe we should take on. According to the theory of self-discrepancy, people can experience a gap between the current life condition and their idea life. Therefore, people's inability to see their aspirations become a reality can lead to frustrations, mild to severe level of anxiety. In other words, some people can go through episodes of identity crisis from experiencing a feeling of self-discrepancy.

Let us use Mark's life story to best illustrate the concept of self-discrepancy. Mark is a salesperson, but he wants to become an expert in training and developing people. He is also seeing someone who pressures him to take the relationship to the next level. Based on the self-discrepancy theory, his actual self is an salesperson; his ideal self is management consultant; and his ought self is to take more responsibility in his personal life.

While some people can effectively manage various domains of the self without experiencing personal identity crisis, others might not be, as a result of that experience episode of crisis. The likelihood of someone to experience an identity crisis is tied to the ability of that person to be self-assured about his or her decisions. Someone who goes after one aspect of himself might face proper level of stress suitable for such a situation and avoid a crisis. Someone who goes after two domains is more likely to face an identity crisis than someone who chooses to change in one domain at a time. Let us look at Mark's scenario, again. He might go through period crisis experience a crisis if he wants to become a management consultant and commit to the relationship at the same time. An attempt to pursuit those two unrelated goals and aspirations might create a significant level of stress or crisis. For example, if Mark fails to recognize his actual or present self, behaves through his ideal self, and acts as though he can do what he believes he ought to do, he is likely to experience episodes of self-discrepancy. Self-discrepancy can be experienced when you fail meet his or her self-perceived expectations.

The quality of your life and level of happiness is in part tied to the clarity of your identity throughout your life. Developing a strong and clear identity is key ingredient to overcome opposing situations. Such situations can and may hinder your aptitude to make sense of your inner self and external environment, to know who you are as a person and as a human being, including the kind of person you are and your potential. The journey of developing a strong and rich identity requires being aware of potential obstacles due to self-perceived expectations.

ILL MATURATION

HEALTHY SENTIMENTS CREATE POSITIVE BEHAVIORS AND ATTITUDES. Unhealthy sentiments create unhealthy behaviors and attitudes. Some unhealthy state of beings is linked to poor reasoning and choice. Other unhealthy state of beings is no fault of us but created by an ill process of maturation. In your journey of wellness and wellbeing, it is important to accept your mental, emotional, and psychological challenges, as opposed to fighting or denying them. You may have nothing to do with some of your predicaments. Life itself is challenging. You may face life's unpredictable events due to poor reasoning. You may also face some obstacles due to no fault of yours. Our abilities to read, write, speak or think, for example, are linked to biological process (e.g. pruning process). A faulty pruning process has direct implications to intellectual aptitude. In other words, ill maturation affects people's learning abilities. For that reason, accepting our life predicaments can be an effective way to get rid of unhealthy sentiments.

Adults are not spared from identity crisis, although they might have already gone thru typical challenging times such as career choice, life partners, and political affiliation. Life's unpredictable events, the fast pace of life or the socioeconomic constraints of this postmodern cause millions of people to be confronted with issues previously dealt at one point over the course of their lives. Therefore, we should be careful to deal with those mundane aspects of life, as opposed to seeing ourselves powerless in the face of life challenges. Some people are not completely exempted from the long-term effect of their past choices, but they are better equipped to face difficult situations.

Simply put, ill maturation can occur within a specific stage or between stages of human growth, irrespective of age groups. Each age group is affected by different factors, though some affect most age groups. Others are unique to some age groups. Behaviors are internalized, so are the images we project in our subconscious mind. Consequently, some people might struggle to develop a strong and rich identity due to their involvement in some antisocial behaviors and activities during childhood.

MAKING LEMONADE OUT OF LEMONS

HAVE YOU EVER HEARD THAT CRISIS IS PART OF LIFE AND YOU WERE somewhat indifferent to that statement? You could have been if you have not yet gone through a similar situation. Those words would certainly resonate to someone who has been there. Part of the good news is that personal crisis is a normal aspect of life and some crises are common among people, regardless of age, gender, race, and walk of life. Existential crisis, for example, is a common human-related crisis many people go through at one point in their life. In the real world, people can have a breakdown for a number of reasons: unknown biological parents, highly dysfunctional home, and long period of unemployment, breakup, divorce, or poor social integration. The main thing is to respond to crisis or obstacle as opposed to reacting to it. When you respond to a situation, you take control of it. When you react to it, you allow it to control you. Reacting is allowing the situation control how you feel and think.

Crisis is an aspect of human's life. But an essential point is to choose to respond to it as opposed to react or feel powerless to it. As a popular saying goes, you may need to consider making "lemonade out of lemons." In conclusion, people can experience periods of crisis for

From a personal standpoint, I have been concerned with self-discrepancy issues, such as how to become what I aspire to be and become the self I see fit. When properly handled, identity crisis can be helpful for people to not only inquiry a little more about who they are, but also recognize their abilities, and sense of worth, reach for attain higher level of productivity, enhance their lifestyle, and live a rewarding, meaningful, and fulfilled life.

Experiencing identity crisis can be a blessing in disguise. It is an opportunity to channel our energy, time, and resources toward what matters most to us in life. It is also an opportunity to make choices you would want to make in an ideal situation. In other words, identity crisis can be an opportunity to take a new direction and transform our life.

Excellence is a better teacher than mediocrity. The lessons of the ordinary are everywhere. Truly profound and original insights are to be found only in studying the exemplary.

—Warren Bennis

My prayer is to learn new things, imbibe fresh insights. You must not take life too seriously. You must enjoy the process of living.

—Sonu Nigam

3

GAINING INSIGHTS

BECOMING THE BEST VERSION REQUIRES DEVELOPING NEW AND FRESH perspectives. Sometimes negative events can hold us back to become a new person. Unless we feed our younger self with fresh and sound perspectives, we might not be able to move past some toxic belief, attitude, and behavior. Becoming the best version of you does not mean forgetting past mistakes, failures, and unpleasant memories. Rather, it means looking at them in new and fresh ways that might help us cope and recover from setbacks and life unpredictable events. It is essential to tackle unwanted memories and events because they carry energies that distort our thinking, feeling and behavior. This chapter offers ways to revisit some unpleasant life situations or missed opportunities from a new and fresh look.

People are resistant to change, which might prevent some people to adapt and do what it is necessary in order evolve. But if you had the opportunity to revisit some of important and crucial moments in your life, would you be willing to learn and alter whatever necessary mentally, emotionally, or psychologically, in order to evolve and be the best of you? Clinical study has shown that techniques such as reflection and retroflection have helped people to regain control of their sense of selves, in a natural and undistorted way.

Sections of this chapter cover proven techniques to help regain and strengthen your sense of self out of life's unwanted events obstacles. One way to recognize whether you are being transformed through practice is when you have new and fresh perspectives toward similar obstacles and problems that might come your way. Moreover, you can assess your progress when you are getting a stronger and richer sense of self. Lastly, you should keep practicing the best version of you, so that you might not feel stuck in your personal or professional life.

INSIGHTS FROM SELF-REFLECTION

SOME EXTERNAL EVENTS MAY NOT ALLOW YOU TO DEVELOP A PROPER personal identity; unfortunately, you find yourself unable to endure stressful situations, set admirable personal values, achieve goals, and live a satisfied life. Many people go through life, unable to recover from setbacks Some people find themselves stuck, confuse, and helplessness. Many people can overcome their challenges and obstacles through the power of self-discovery. You can further knowledge of you and your life through self-reflection. Making time for soul-searching and self-examination offers several valuable benefits. For example, in soul-searching, you look at several factors, just like trying to make sense of the overall condition, including situations in life. a life condition can be described as a permanent state, a situation can be described as an event in life. Soul-searching and self-examination help people to not only revisit past and previous events but also to view them from fresh angles. Life is lived through external and internal forces. Life is a combination of what is seen and unseen. The daily routine and the pressures of life may be among the reasons preventing you to understand yourself better. Still, you can build a solid and rich knowledge about not only who or what you are, but also how you can diversify your set of skills and abilities, as a human being.

People who have never experienced a crisis might miss the opportunity to develop a strong and rich sense of selves. But they can still do it through a process of self-examination. Self-examination offers the opportunity to analyze lived experiences through various lenses.

RETROFLECTING ON IMPORTANT EVENTS

YOU CAN REGAIN YOUR SENSE OF SELF AND BUILD YOUR LIFE UP THROUGH retroflection. In simple terms, retroflection is like a positive projection. Rather than looking at unpleasant life experience through blame and regret, you look at them with the purpose to alter a specific behavior, beliefs, sentiment, or line of thinking. In other words, retroflection is reconnecting to your younger self in a positive way.

Now, go over one or two events in your life in a constructive and positive viewpoint, using the lines below.

....

....

....

....

LOSING THE BATTLE BUT WINNING THE WAR

ONE OF THE LESSONS THE WORLD HAS LEARNED FROM WORLD WAR II IS that losing a battle does not mean losing a war. We can observe that phenomenon at play in sports. For example, in boxing, a fighter can lose one or two rounds, but ends up winning the fight. Sometimes in life, we must take on battles we did not anticipate and if we get knock down it does not mean a comeback is out of the equation. Usually, the fight is over when one fighter concedes and calls it off. But until then, the fight is still on and victory may be a reality. A good thing about life's obstacles is that the life we have within is greater than the obstacles we face. Problems are contextual, restrained in scope, and limited by time. You can choose to stay the course and fight until you get what they want.

When we go through setbacks, there are things we can do to help ourselves to get back on our feet. First, it is crucial to recognize the situation at hand, in order to have a clear understanding of it. Secondly, problems can cause us to panic and lose our sense of self. Therefore, we need to be in a state of serenity or calmness, not because everything is all right, but because we need a sound mind to make sound decisions, particularly in difficult time. Next, we need to identity the outcome we want. In order words, what is it that you want out of the situation? You might not be able to solve a problem if you do not know the outcome you want. You may be left confused, stuck and defeated during adversity, without a clear idea of what you want. Lastly, we need to be positive and inspired in order to attain what we want. Let us look at those points from a chapter of World War II.

RECOGNIZING THE SITUATION. When France was melting down under the German's army during World War II, the French Army General, Charles de Gaulle was not in denial about the situation. He recognized the France was under siege by the Germans. He sought refuge in England and during that retreat; he was able to assess the situation. He realized that France's defeat had major implications in other European's nations. Similarly, a French victory meant a lot for other countries. He also recognized many French civilians were willing to help the French army to get back on its feet. We too, when we experience setbacks, we can turn things around by understanding our predicament, recognizing what it is at stake, and relying on our support system.

In times of challenge and hardship you need to recognize the importance of the moment and what matter the most to you and people you care for. Those elements can help you be up to the challenge, take the right course of action on your own. You can rely on people's support while playing a leadership role. Success is for you to make it happen, not anybody else.

STAYING CALM. When we face obstacles, it can be easy to not see the situation for what it is for various reasons. For example, some people might panic. Some people might exaggerate the situation. Other people might just fight back, as a defense mechanism. Although, human's first instinct is fight-flight, we can choose to respond instead of reacting to problems. Staying calm allows us to see a problem for what it is and respond to it from a place of wholeness, as opposed to fear. In a state of serenity, we can also deal with our obstacles from a place of strength, using all that we have for the outcome we want.

For example, the French general, Charles de Gaulle changed the course of a war that was fought on the ground and air from a place of retreat. He did that by making a speech on BBC's network. His sense of serenity helped him to identify and implement unconventional ways to respond to the situation. You too can have fresh ideas and alternative solutions to your adversity, from a place of calmness and serenity.

DEFINING THE OUTCOME. When facing difficult situation, you might not be able to succeed without knowing in advance the outcome you want. From the famous speech of June 1940s, "France [may have] lost a battle, but France has not lost the war", France and its allies were able to anticipate an outcome they desperately wanted. That speech delivered by the French Army general did not only boost the morale in France, but it also allowed people from other countries to consider the idea of France winning over the German's army. Some historians suggested Winston Churchill found Charles de Gaulle's speech remarkable and strategic. In short, setbacks can be times of new beginnings. You should have a clear idea of the outcome you want. Not identifying a desirable outcome in the face of obstacle may be disadvantageous. Identifying one can be empowering and inspiring.

BE POSITIVE AND INSPIRED. Unhappiness, giving up, and giving in might not get you close to what you want in life. In challenging times, being positive can be beneficial. One way to be positive is belief that those hardships are temporary, as opposed to a permanent. You can also celebrate small victories and be inspired by them, as opposed to discounting the small progress you make. As a Chinese saying goes, "a journey of a thousand miles begins with a single-step." When we are positive the universe will lead us to greater things. For example, being positive and inspired for a greater good helped France and its allies to resist and find ways to win the war. Charles de Gaulle stayed optimistic and believed the French army could regain control over the situation. The Prime Minister, Winston Churchill thought of Charles de Gaulle as a man of destiny because the world was in better place.

In conclusion, amid obstacles and adversities, you can come in terms with your predicaments. That can put you in better state of mind. Becoming aware of the current situation, it is like opening yourself up for fresh ideas and new perspectives, which might lead you to outcome beyond your expectations. New beginnings can be about strengthening your sense of self, setting personal boundaries, finding your own voice; giving a meaning to what you have; reconnecting with your family; connecting with new people; or giving yourself another chance. In short, new beginnings are about going after your hopes, dreams and aspirations for your well-being and that of people the community, in which you live, pray, work, and play.

CHANGING THE DYNAMICS

I N ONE POINT IN TIME, I WAS NOT HAPPY ABOUT MY LIFE AND I DECIDED TO DO whatever necessary to change its course. The idea of changing the environment seemed to be an effective way to alter my way of life, including my psychological state of mind. I relocated to another state, eager for a new and fresh start. Personal transformation begins with changing the forces at work in my daily affairs.

Fortunately, that decision has helped me find my voice through fresh beliefs, values, and clear aspirations. Becoming the best version of self requires changing the dynamics at hands and the way you go about your life. You may not need to relocate to alter the direction of your life, including its dynamic, you can identify ways that fit you best.

YOUR TURN. Reflect on your life for a little moment, particularly on an area that you desperately want to be better. Reflect on your values. List some of the things that you could do to improve it, without giving much thought into it. You may write your ideas on the lines bellow. Feel free to get a notebook or an extra sheet of paper.

....

....

....

....

....

....

....

....

....

....

....

....

....

....

....

....

....

....

....

REFRAMING LIFE'S EVENTS

K NOWING THE DIRECTION OF YOUR LIFE IS AN IMPORTANT FACTOR FOR living a purposeful and meaningful life. In your journey of making sense of your life, you should rely on truths rather than unhealthy feelings, negative thoughts, and people's opinions that did not help you become the best version of you.

Unhealthy mindset, negative thoughts, bad memories, and regrets are nothing but weights and burdens, which prevent us to live a happy, successful, and passionate life. One way to remove unnecessary weights of your life is to look at those events using a new set of lenses. Reframing an event is looking at it from a new and fresh way, as opposed to dwelling on pain, regrets, and hurts. it is said that our perception is our reality. Therefore, if we look at some events from a different viewpoint, the new perception can become our reality. Events are all about thinking and feeling. If you change how you think about something, you have a different feeling about that same thing. You can free yourself from regrets and pains by changing your thinking and feeling.

PERSONAL EXAMPLE. Here was my attempt to rewrite my life story based on truths to free my mind and to break away from the emotional and psychological weight that comes with unexpected life events.

As earlier mentioned, when I newly arrived in the United States, I had drifted away from the true purpose

----

of my trip and ended facing major unexpected life events. I came to the United States alone to get a better life through higher education. I had not plan to pursue that dream with someone else, in my life. It was a venture that needed to be taken alone. Though things went unplanned, the trip did not completely go south.

I ended up earning the highest degree in Higher Education, a doctorate degree, an achievement beyond my expectations. I have also uncovered my authorship competency, a childhood aspiration—another self-realization beyond my wildest dream. I have never contemplated the possibility of turning that idea into a reality, until I came to the United States. Most importantly, taking the time to examine my beliefs, values, and aspirations has been a significant step toward reconnecting with who I am, my ideal self, and matters important to me.

The events that caused me to drift away from my ambition are nothing but "parentheses" in my life. Those events are opportunities, to remember who I have become and celebrate my successes unapologetically. The adversity of life can be vehicles to go after long-held dreams and aspirations buried by forces beyond control.

YOUR TURN. Dr. Jordan Peterson, a professor of psychology and a clinical psychologist claims one of the simple ways to start a project is to do it poorly. It sounds weird at first, but it is a great way to start doing what seems discomforting or annoying. So, use that approach to rewrite some aspects of your life in a way, to appear encouraging and confident. Steve Jobs explained that it is only when you look back in your life that some events make sense. Use the space provided below to write about your life and look at it from a new and fresh angle.

FINDING YOUR NORTH POLE IN DIFFICULT TIME

YOUR SENSE OF SELF AND PERSONAL AMBITION ARE CONNECTED TO YOUR true north. When you lose sight of things you aspire to is like shifting away from the north pole of life. You can feel lost, stuck and be unable to make sense of your life, relationships, and seize some opportunities that come your way, when you are not tune to your true north. You have a sense of direction in life, guided by who you are and what you are at a specific moment in your life. That dynamic or feeling that you have comes from a place, a destination. That place is your pole north. We all have a pole north. When we are in the range of the frequency of our pole north, we feel secure, optimist, happy, and genuine. When we are out of its range, we might wander, feel stuck or unable to become who we aspire to be.

PERSONAL EXAMPLE. For example, when I decided to come to the United States, my main goal was to make a way create a path to my professional life through education. I was eager for it. I had the intellectual and socioeconomic capital for it, which gave me the confidence that I could turn my dream into a reality. But soon after I arrived, I had to face the unpredictable: I went through three interrelated traumatic events. Culture shock, breakup, and no support from my parents. For me, the culture shock had to do with the fast pace of life and the level of assertiveness. Americans are straight to the point and pay less attention to nonverbal communication. I also experienced a breakup with someone I was with in Africa. I had her come to the U.S against my parents' approval. Breaking up with her made me loss my inner connection with home. Within a relative short period, I lost the blessings of my parents because of romantic aspiration. My main aspiration was no longer my priority, although it was still important to me. I was no longer in tuned with my aspirations and the obstacles I faced were not those related to my true goals and aspirations. I had become mentally, emotionally, and psychologically unfit to live up to my destiny, because I had channel those energies where they were not meant to be.

Life cannot be lived without obstacles. However, people usually have what it takes to succeed. It can be harder to overcome some obstacles when we do not face the right set of challenges and obstacles. For example, we can face the wrong kind of obstacles when we are not aligned with our aspirations and when we do not go after our goals. In other words, our everyday life must reflect what we aspire to so that our actions and energies must be aligned with what we aim for, in a near or distant future.

Back to my story, culture shock could not be avoided and was a sure thing to happen. But reuniting with a significant person is not a matter one cannot control. Fortunately, I was able still interested in my personal development and achieving my professional goals. My interest in personal growth had allowed me to reconnect with my inner being and to pay attention to it. My eagerness to succeed in my professional life had helped to realize that although I had been able to achieve academic goals and aspirations, things did not feel right. I felt like I was just wandering around with my life.

Our aspirations are products of our imaginations and state of beings. My state of being was not aligned with my aspirations, despite my achievements. Scientists explain that the North Pole is a specific geographic area located on the northern hemisphere of the earth. But a magnetic pole can be anywhere on the surface of the earth. In that zone the needle of a magnetic compass points people toward the north pole, but it might be the right direction. In other words, when you are geographically located in that area a magnetic compass can potentially be misleading. Subsequently, you can find yourself wandering around, stuck, and not making good use of your energies and resources.

In everyday life, you may let to believe that you are living your best life, especially when you have been able to achieve what you have set to do. However, you can be successful and still be unfulfilled. That feeling of emptiness calls for a need to recognize and live up to what your life and successes mean to you. In other words, that feeling of emptiness call for your true north, a place that gives meaning to your aspirations, a place that gives you satisfaction and infinite value. You might say it is place where that allows you to leave the world better place than you found it.

You may be in search for your true north when, despite your successes and accomplishments, you feel unsatisfied and in need of something that seems reachable, but also seems unreachable for reasons not easy to explain. Many people at the executive level of major organizations feel unsatisfied inwardly, despite their professional successes. For that reason, the field of executive coaching stresses on personal growth and make a connection to day-to-day work life.

For many people, work takes over all areas of their life. That social phenomenon is common across industries and professions. One way to understand the large picture of that phenomenon is to recognize that in a Capitalistic market environment as well as in collective market environment, working people are perceived as means of production. In the absence of an effective piece of equipment, labor is needed, at the expense of people wellness and wellbeing. job experts say, "you are hired for your skills and fired for your behavior." At the individual level, it can useful to be aware that human competency deficiency can be translated through self-inflicted injuries, which can be physical, emotional, and psychological.

To conclude with my story, despite of my academic accomplishments and promising professional life. My life was not aligned with my North Pole, my aspirations in life, although I was doing well in both areas. Inside of me I felt unfulfilled. I also felt like I was wandering around with a blurred sense of self, and unclear vision. After repetitive reflection, I was realized two things. My state of being was not in sync with my successes. Therefore, my true self struggled to be in tune with my aspirations or North Pole. It was like I was in a magnetic zone as opposed to the North Pole.

PART 2

SELF-ACTUALIZATION AND SELF-REALIZATION

It is easy to do good, but it takes a lifetime to become human!

—AainaA-Ridtz A R

We are all butterflies. Earth is our chrysalis.

—LeeAnn Taylor

4

WHAT TYPE OF PERSON ARE YOU?

THE TYPE OF PERSON THAT YOU ARE CAN BE REVEALED THROUGH your personal qualities. Touching on the Big Five personality traits based on the work of Isabel Briggs Myers and Katharine Cook Briggs, to other major concepts that stress on social and professional qualities. describe human behavior such as *Machiavellianism, narcissism, self-monitoring,* and *proactive personality*, this chapter covers classic*(Machiavellianism)* and modern day*(self-monitoring* and *proactive) qualities,* that can help you understand what type of person who might want to "model" from. It can be difficult to differentiate the personality attributes that are socially oriented from those that are business-oriented because they go hand in hand, especially in a workplace setting.

Personality type is one of the most popular bases commonly used to understand oneself and other people's traits. The concept of personality is not employed by psychology researchers, as it is among ordinary people.

For an ordinary person, understanding the concept of personality is limited to traits, such as agreeableness, openness, or extraversion. For experts in psychology, variability is perceived as a dynamic idea describing the development and growth of a person's whole psychological system. In the community, it is not only about a person's traits or characteristics, but also about a person's biological and psychological abilities to adapt to a milieu. To further illustrate the difference, while the ordinary person makes sense of his behavior, interacts with others, and reacts under pressure, behavioral psychology experts go beyond those factors. In addition to hereditary factors, experts include the general environment and one's specific capabilities to adapt. There are implications in those two viewpoints. For example, attempting to understand who you are based on your personality traits can be like understanding oneself at the surface, primarily because human identity has several layers. Consequently, a narrow understanding about what type of person that you are can get stuck, feel confused, and be ineffective.

One important factor that has contributed in advancing the study of personality-traits can be understood from the words of Myers, a pioneer of the concept. She explained that "when people differ, knowledge of type lessens friction and eases discomfort among people. No one has to be good at everything." Those words encapsulate best the main idea behind the work of Briggs and Myers. Research progress in personality has been undertaken from the premise that the concept can be a significant basis to help people understand their nature with the goal to minimize conflict among them and celebrate human attitudes. Findings on the subject have been valuable. Based on the work of Myers and Briggs, for instance, an ordinary person can understand every day personality traits, such as *extroverted* (outgoing) vs. *introverted* (reserved), *sensing* (practical) vs. *intuiting* (abstract), *judging* (structure) vs. *perceiving* (flexible), or *thinking* (logic) vs. *feeling* (value). The mother–daughter team (Briggs and Myers) has helped laypeople to understand and appreciate differences in personalities, in a healthy and harmonious way, particularly in social and business settings. But understanding what type of person you are only from the standpoint of the work of Briggs and Myers might be narrowed.

PROFESSIONAL QUALITIES

OTHERS ATTITUDE-BASED RESEARCH ENDEAVORS HAVE SHED LIGHT ON people's behaviors and lifestyle in the context of the workplace and business. The next paragraphs take a close look at some of those research findings.

MACHIAVELLIANISM. One classic example of the research is the work of Niccolò Machiavelli, which is traced back in the 16th century. Machiavelli's work stresses on pragmatism, emotional distance, assertiveness, and persuasion, as well as the desire to win by "all means." In today's competitive and highly demanding socioeconomic environment, those qualities are essential in the world of business and everyday life. Many people usually express are unenthusiastic about the work of Machiavellianism, partly, because of some people tend to think of the main as radical person who would do whatever necessary to get the outcome he wants. Some people would think of him as manipulator, greedy, and corrupt. Unless one is practical, emotionally intelligent, assertive, and persuasive, you might not be an effective and achieve your goal. Machiavelli's framework can be beneficial to everyone if one has clear boundaries.

PERSONALITY TYPE. Another valuable attribute to describe behavior in an organization is the *personality type*, which is a useful premise to make sense of a socioeconomic environment. The literature of the concept indicates two personality types: Type A and Type B. A material from the Association Talent Development (ATD, formerly known as the ASTD) includes a big picture, but insightful description of four personality types at the organizational level: charismatic, analytical, friendly, and the achiever.

You are a **Charismatic** person if you are habitually

- Persuasive
- Adventurous
- Energetic
- Creative, but somewhat disorganized

You are **Analytical** if you are consistently

- Logical
- Detail-oriented
- Methodical
- Slow decision-makers

You are an **Achiever** if you are consistently

- Inquisitive
- Goal-oriented
- Energetic and somewhat impatient
- Fast learner

From a broad standpoint, Type A refers to the socioeconomic dimension and the way of life in a traditional, individualistic society such as what we have in the United States. In such competitive and dense environment, people are highly driven by goals and ambition; individual welfare takes over collective interest. You would describe a Type A personality as people who

- Walk, work, eat, and speak fast
- Tend to be multitaskers
- Work long hours
- Allocate little time for personal leisure
- Tend to be highly competitive

In contrast, you will describe yourself as Type B personality if you show at two of these qualities

- Flexible and tolerant
- Likely to delegate
- Easily connecting with people
- Less likely to be stressed out
- Responsive to having fun and relaxation
- Inclined to be satisfied in life

PROACTIVE PERSONALITY. Recent research indicates that some people tend to find balance between those two main personality types. Experts refer to it as *proactive personality* and people with that attribute tend to

- Take initiatives
- Identify opportunities
- Develop contact in high places
- Possess the right mental abilities related to specific tasks
- Possess the right emotional and psychological stamina
- Create positive change
- Behave and act like a leader

The concept of personality is deemed useful in developing a balanced, healthy, and favorable self-identity; research based on the concept has been primarily driven to help people understand their own behavior, assert preferences, and become tolerant of attitudes that might differ from those that are normally considered acceptable. Most importantly, the concept has been useful for people, including you and me, to be aware of and develop proper behavior and attitude in response to the diverse circumstances and areas of their life (personal and professional); there is value to that aspect mainly because our personality traits shed light on the type of people that we are.

In summary, the focus of conventional understanding of what type of person that you are is based on the idea of personality, primarily influenced by the work of Briggs and Myers. One of the main reasons is that their work makes the subject relatable and less complex. But, one of the main goals of their work was to encourage people to be open-minded and tolerant. The purpose of this section of the book has been to encourage the readers to go beyond the conventional understanding of personality. Most importantly to further your understanding of what type of person that you believe to be, based on your intrinsic and extrinsic factors. You are also encouraged to distinguish qualities from attributes. Quality, as a trait that you may have developed and used when necessary, as opposed to attribute, an intrinsic trait that may not have gained but developed for mastery.

Don't aim for success if you want it; just do what you love and believe in, and it will come naturally.

—David Frost

It's not what other people believe you can do, it's what you believe.

—Gail Devers

5

WHAT CAN YOU DO?

B ECOMING YOUR BEST VERSION IS ALSO ABOUT BE WELL-AWARE OF WHAT you can do and how you can rise to the level of your potential. One way to do it is by focusing on what you do well. In psychology jargon, doing what you do best is referred to be in your "zone", a place where time stands still, because most of your human energies is channeled toward what you do. Doing what you do best is not a popular mindset and easy to execute due to forces that appear to be outside of our control. Becoming the best of you in professional life requires taking roads less taken. Financial strategist experts explain that 1 to 10 % of the wealthy demographic do well because they earn money based on how they think, as opposed to what they do. Most people trade their time for money: Some of them get paid by the hour and others get paid by what they do. About 10% of people get paid because of how they think.

Once you know what you do well, like everyone, you can rely on the concept of goal setting to be effective. Most people function well by setting goals, which makes it easy for an ordinary person to be motivated. For example, academic goals allow students to work hard, get high grade, or complete their programs. Setting goals drives the productivity level of salespeople. People have goals, but not many get to achieve them. Several factors are involved in determining the success of individuals in the scenarios. They have accepted their attributes (i.e., as student or professional). More specifically, they were able to recognize their qualities (e.g., cognitive aptitude) and potentials (e.g., self-determination or persistence).

You too can achieve your goals, live the lifestyle you want, enter the profession, or get a promotion you have been hoping for through clear-thinking. Research study tells us that we are not a static being, but an evolving being in almost every aspect of life, including our mind, as research in neuroplasticity explains. Therefore, you can do and achieve whatever you have not been able to previously because you may have learned, done, experienced things that might have make you a smarter, wiser, and more informed person. You may have also purposefully reflected on new and fresh ways to put in practice concepts, processes, and principles in order to succeed in whatever areas of interest in your life. One of the determining factors of your aptitude is developing a strong and rich sense of who you are. Developing a clear sense of self is like empowering self toward new heights.

IDENTITY CLARITY IS AN ASSET

PART OF HUMAN DEVELOPMENT IS TO HONE OUR SENSE OF SELF, INCLUDING our identity. That process, which begins from childhood to adulthood, has a direct effect in our ability to showcase our gifts, talents, and skills. In other words, our sense of self is at the core of a successful professional life. While some people, early on in their life get a clear sense of who they are, other people live without a clear sense of self. Not having a sense of self has direct effect in our professional life.

SUCCEEDING IN WHAT YOU DO. Someone from whom we can learn about how our sense of self, including our identity may influence our professional life is Erik Erikson. You can learn from him, not only because he is considered a pioneer in the study of personal identity, but also because of his lived experience. For example, at some point in his life, he struggled to succeed in his professional life because while grew up, he was made to believe that his stepfather was his biological father. That lie had adverse consequences in his aptitude due to the fact his mom and stepfather kept from vital information relevant to his personal identity and sense of self. During his apprenticeship in art, Erikson did so poorly, and it occurred to him his poor sense of self stood as obstacle his inability to do well in his traineeship. Erikson experienced an *identity crisis*, a concept he introduced. He devoted the rest of his life study in psychology and psychoanalysis, after recovering from his own personal identity crisis. The lack of self-confidence is a leading cause of underperformance and underemployment. One of the most essential ingredients for people to succeed in their occupation is their sense of self, including how they hold themselves within themselves in everyday life.

If you struggle with self-confidence and have not considered the theory of self-identity, you should. One conventional way to develop self-confidence is to focus on skills set. However, sometimes the real problem is not about what you know and can do, but whether you can hold yourself within yourself. In everyday jargon, you may consider "getting yourself together", in the sense of being in the present moment.

Sometimes, you might be able to stay in the present moment and therefore struggle to develop a strong and rich sense of self. Dramatic events, including those experienced as far back as in our childhood might stand as hurdle to become who want to be. Living the present moment can difficult due to our unwanted lived experiences. But it is worth applying one's self to it.

A clear sense of personal identity can get you unstuck and help you to move forward Erikson's life story illustrates best such scenario. Before making a name for himself in the field of psychology, he was interested in art, but lacked confidence to excel in it due to an unclear personal identity. With a deep interest in developing a clear identity, he was able to regain control over his personal life and became a recognized psychanalysis researcher, though he had no formal academic training on the subject.

Reflecting on the self-identity can be liberating and empowering. In a fast-pace and ever-changing socioeconomic environment, such as that of the United States, many people choose to enter a line of work just because it is convenient for them or the job pays well. The problem with that reasoning is that most people have an uncultivated knowledge about their own potentials and life purpose. They may also underestimate the effect of living a life based on preference, instead of what is available or less difficult to obtain. Although opportunities abound, not all of them are good; some might not even be the right fit for you. Usually, the right opportunities are a good match in terms of preferences (you easily get in your zone). If you are aware of your potentials, but you take a position under your professional credential, then you are likely to be in that job for a short time.

DO NOT LIVE TO WORK, BUT WORK TO LIVE. If you are aware of your work-related qualities, including potential, and have a job, but are struggling with self-confidence, then you are not probably holding a job that suitable for you. Additional training and development can be helpful but might not significantly eliminate the issue. If you do not enjoy what you do, it does not matter how much experience you accumulate; you are still underperforming based on your natural qualities and potentials. Our behavior is an aspect of our attitude, which reflects our perception and emotion. If you accept a job offer, which you do not like, though you act like you do, your attitude will ultimately betray you. The point is: Be aware of your qualities and self-worth so that you make sound choices in your professional life. Work should help become the best of your authentic self.

If you want to reach and maximize your full potential and be satisfied in your professional life, then revisiting some troubling events that occurred early in your life can be part of the solution. Most challenges and difficulties people face in their work and life are related not only to their recent events, but also to some episodes of their childhood and adolescence. Usually, the opportunity to develop a firm sense of self occurs during the adolescence stage of human development. It is not anymore, a secret that many people recognize that their parents, spouses, or close friends' expectations can significantly influence career choices and levels of achievement. Those who can make the most important life decisions on their own are usually satisfied and successful in their professional life, including personal life.

Reflecting on your self-identity can help you to assert your preference, hopes, and aspiration. For example, based on the theory of self, your personality can be under the influence of "me" or "I." "Me" tends to take over the self, when it comes to social expectations ingrained in you since your early childhood. "I" in self is your ability to develop a sound mind. When you stay focused in the moment so that you can make good judgment, even for matters of the future, you are giving or making room for "I" in self. With "I," you can be flexible, creative, and interdependent in your professional life. It is also open to win-win outcomes. With "me," you can only cooperate, be satisfied with win–lose outcomes, and find lose–lose results acceptable.

When we do not have a strong and rich sense of who we are, we can still function, but unfulfilled. We can also be successful but dissatisfied. Many of us manage to go to work every day despite the pressures of life. We manage to be at work on time, beat the traffic or the weather, and use lunch break to make quick phone calls. Yet, within us, we feel as though there is more to life than that daily routine. Although we can function in the environment in which we live, work, and play, that does not necessarily mean we feel fulfilled. Experiencing that feeling of satisfaction cannot be found in our ability to complete our daily routine, but in having a strong and rich sense of who we are, what we are, and what we can do.

Most people are other people. Their thoughts are someone else's opinions, their lives a mimicry, their passions a quotation.

—Oscar Wilde

When I discover who I am, I'll be free.

—Ralph Ellison, *Invisible Man*

6

WHO AM I?

"**W**HO AM I? IS QUESTION COMMONLY DISCUSSED AND PERCEIVED through everyday lenses such as hereditary factors, such as life's events, gender, personality traits, physical appearance, ethnicity, faith, and occupation. Although these factors offer valuable information about who we are as an individual, they do not shed little light toward understanding our self in a holistic manner. The question "who am I" need to be address beyond basic characteristics. This chapter examines that question through several lenses: Psychiatry, sociology, and psychology. It goes beyond the conventional lens of the Big Five personality types.

THE BIG FIVE PERSONALITY TRAITS

THE IDEA OF PERSONALITY CAN BE A USEFUL CONCEPT OF DEVELOPING A rich and strong self-identity. Research based on the concept has been primarily driven in describing behavior, positive social qualities related to workplace and organizational purpose. However, forming and developing a comprehensive sense of personal identity should be done beyond the boundary of personality traits such as the Big-Five approach. Many people wear various kinds of emotional or personality "masks" to strive and navigate challenges and obstacles in life. Some people might be able to do well, without any significant adverse consequences; other people might find themselves unable to function from a position of authentic self. The impostor syndrome, for example, is a typical personality problem many people in modern and postmodern society struggle against in a day-to-day life, whether they are in the classroom, office cubicle, boardroom, kitchen table, or place of prayer.

A strong and rich understanding who we are as a human and person requires several perspectives. After all, self-discover and self-awareness are like a hermeneutic phenomenological inquiry and questions of related to self-identity are best understood based on the lived experiences. The life story of Erik Erikson illustrates best that idea. In a quest to understand who he was as a human being, Erikson overcame identity crisis without previous academic and formal training on self-concept; he educated himself on the discipline and made scholarly contribution to the field.

The emphasis of personality-based research is primarily on behavior and attitude. However, these aspects are only helpful in describing a single dimension of who we are, as a person and as a human being. A study in psychology, for instance, indicates that personality-based research can be misleading mainly because it lacks focus on the unconscious dimension of our human nature. Understanding who we are involves more from the angle of personality that a sense of self. In fact, the Big Five personality traits are best described through the acronym O.C.E.A.N (Openness, Consciousness, Extroverted, Agreeable, and Neuronal). Study on that frame of work can be helpful to understand behavior and attitude in social and business contexts, in order to be develop social capital and successful in our professional life. Nonetheless the Big Five personality traits can valuable in becoming aware of individual behavior and attitude, although it does not further our understanding about our ideal self and authentic self. Therefore, it might be useful to consider alternatives frame of works related to understand our ideal self and cultivate our authentic self.

USING PSYCHIATRIC LENS

RESEARCH IN PSYCHIATRY SHOWS THAT HOW WE BEHAVE, FEEL, AND THINK are a major part of who we are as human beings. But sometimes, how we behave, feel, and think might not allow our sense of self to show and shine as we would like to. Feeling unsecured, afraid, ridiculed or judged are some of the emotion that might work against of sense of self and feeling of well-being. Our true self is authentic, present, enthusiastic, and alive. But sometimes in severe cases some people perceive a discrepancy between their true being and what they experience emotionally. The concept of personality mask has been proven to best understand how we behave, feel, and think in everyday life, using a psychiatric lens.

In the United States, each year, the last day of October Is Halloween, a national holiday. Families across the nation disguise themselves by donning costumes. On that day, parents accompany their children in the neighborhood, knocking on houses to collect candies. According to major news outlets, such as the *New York*

Times and *Forbes*, Americans spend several billions of dollars on candy alone. In fact, $9.1 billion was injected in the U.S. economy toward celebrating that tradition, in 2017. During the major event, festivalgoers essentially wear face masks to disguise and protect themselves against bad spirits. On that day, people could become a favorite character. In other words, people could become who or what they desire to be. For some, the occasion is an opportunity to show their true selves and for others, to become their false. In both scenarios, they get the impostor syndrome. The syndrome tends to be a bittersweet feeling to some people, although it can be an opportunity to become who or what they want to be for a brief period. The momentary aspect of it makes it bitter, but the sweet part is that they get to experience what they want, which can be gratifying.

Halloween is a major holiday in the United States. It is celebrated not just because people want to make a point about the need to keep evil spirits away, but also to impersonate a character or take on a persona that they admire. Behavior and attitudes come with implications. Wearing masks indicates people's interest in exploring and examining their personalities, including who they are, as a person and as a human being. The impersonation of favorite character underscores the complex nature of the personal identity and the challenge related to developing a clear self-identity. Next, the amount of resources (time, money, and energy) people allocate to the tradition might not only indicate a personal identity crisis, which is a normal aspect of human existence, but also a common need within a population to develop a strong and rich understanding of who they are and of what they can achieve in life.

In fact, most people wear masks to create a sense of normality and harmony in their professional and social lives. They might wear masks to escape from challenges, obstacles, and setbacks or because they are afraid to let their light shine. In both scenarios, personality's masks cannot only get people confused, stuck, and insecure, but it can also prevent them from discovering their true self and attain stages of self-actualization and self-realization.

USING SOCIOLOGICAL LENS

THE VARIABLE OF PERSONALITY HAS BEEN WIDELY EMBRACED IN MAINSTREAM society because, it is less complex to understand, and it's been an effective approach to predict behavior based on attributes. But it does not shed enough light in the intrapersonal aspect of people, as it relates to their relationship with themselves. In other words, knowledge about the concept of personality has been limited to an outward dimension with little emphasis on inward dynamic.

According to recent studies, every year in the United States, about 19% of adults experience anxiety disorder, 6.8% undergo a depressive disorder, and 8% have substance use disorder. Eating disorder across ages is also major problem. Mental health experts agree those illness have a direct effect on people mental and emotional wellness. Most importantly, research is clear on the diagnosis. Majority of the people who experience one or some mental problems have low self-identity. Many people who suffer from chronic anxiety, depression, or weak willpower have lost sense of who they are and what they can do. Some of the common coping strategies toward recovery include self-esteem, self-care, and encouraging peer influence. Through conventional coping strategies, experts and practitioners acknowledge that part of the solution to the problem is to offer new and fresh lenses from which the affected individuals can see themselves.

Consequently, people's understanding of who they are is mainly limited to one dimension. Using a sociological standpoint, ordinary people can significantly improve the quality of their life, including their mental health. Research in sociology shows that people are not born with a specific self, instead a self that grows over time through two paradigms: "me" (influencing by the environment) and "I" (asserting the characteristics of self).

USING PSYCHOLOGICAL LENS

THERE IS A WEALTH OF KNOWLEDGE ON THE SUBJECT OF PERSONALITY FROM THE lens of psychology, which is helpful for people to develop a strong and clear self-identity. That bank of knowledge about personality can be helpful for people to shed light on their self-identities.

"Who am I?" is a basic and fundamental existential question commonly asked among people across ages. We are not static beings and therefore we likely to face and respond to our sense of self. We are also likely to ask that question when facing fortunate or unfortunate life events. The subject of self-identity is complex. Answering the question "Who am I?" involves factors, such as character and personality.

Let us highlight the difference between character and personality. Both are part of someone's personality. Character outlasts personality. Your personality is likely to change over time, but not your character. It is an essential aspect of your authentic self. Your character does not easily change in our life as personality does. For instance, let us look at the natural stages of human development. Our personality in childhood, adolescence, or young adulthood might not be the same, as we go through the stages of human development. Throughout those stages, we are likely to espouse different behaviors, while our character is likely to be unchanged. Personality is more about how we connect with the outside world.

Another common factor that alters personality is peer influence. Among teenagers, for example, the phenomenon of peer pressure yields many of them into deviant behavior and activities, such as the use of illegal drugs, school cheating, and lying to parents or guardians. Many of those behavior and activities can change their personality but not necessarily their character.

IDENTITY: PERSONAL OR SOCIAL FACTOR?

ALMOST EVERY ONE OF US CAN RELATE TO THESE WORDS AT ONE POINT over the course of life: "Tell me about yourself." You have probably heard about it many times over the course of life and in several occasions, such as, perhaps, when seeking employment or when answering a personal profile in a dating website. Usually, we find ourselves not knowing where to start, what to say, or not to include in our response to that open-ended question. It's uncomfortable to some degree when asked to talk about ourselves. One of the reasons is that our mind has been used to thinking about every day, general information such as name, age, education level, family ties, hobbies, or goals. How we perceive ourselves is generally tied to our family heritage and the environment in which we live. Consequently, we are susceptible to describe who we are based on social factors. However, to the words of Aristotle, "Knowing yourself is the beginning of all wisdom." Aristotle's life story helps us understand when to define our self-identity based on our characters and our environment, including the world around.

Much can be learned about character from Aristotle life's story. The death of Aristotle's father, a Macedonia King's physician, prompted him to enroll at Plato's Academy, in Athens. Note that Plato was Socrates student-scholar and Aristotle had become Plato's brightest student. Aristotle's sense of self gave him the confidence to challenge Plato's, on a regular basis, when he believed his line of reasoning was flawed. That attitude prevented him to lead the Academy after Plato passed away. Consequently, the position was offered to Plato's nephew, recognized to be academically inferior to Aristotle.

Several years later, Aristotle accepted Alexander the Great father's request to tutor his 13 years old son, at the time. Over the years, Aristotle made significant in disciplines such as poetics, logic, psychology, biology, astronomy, and physics. Mostly importantly, he extensively wrote about metaphysics, a branch of philosophical study of principles behind concepts such as substance, knowing, time, space, cause, and identity. Is it by coincidence that Alexander the Great had conquered most of the world known to mankind? He did not allow people to define who he might become. He had a strong and rich sense of self. I'd to believe that he was ambition and guided by principles.

Essential existential questions such as "Who are you?" "What type of person are you?" and "What can you do?" though distinctive, are not separate, but intertwined. While "who you are"(the nature of your being) and "what you are" (the nature of your character) emerge as independent variables of our identity, "what you can do"(skills, abilities, and potential) emerges as a dependent variable. In other words, who we believe we are shapes what we believe, and we do. In addition, what we believe we can do also shape who we believe we are. Lastly, what we believe we are is also at the center of our character, which cannot be easily altered.

To put it all together, if you are interested in becoming the best version of you, you need to consider using several angles. One angle may help you, but it might be narrow. For example, developing your self-identity from one angle offers a narrow understanding about who you represent for your parents, family, relatives, and community members. A single lens of understanding what you can do might also keep you from unlocking your potentials, as well as becoming a prosperous person in life. Conversely, developing a self-identity using several lenses offer stronger and richer sense of self.

PART 3

BECOMING THROUGH SELF-ACCEPTANCE

Wanting to be someone else is a waste of the person you are.

—Marilyn Monroe

You are imperfect, permanently and inevitably flawed. And you are beautiful.

—Amy Bloom

7

MASTERING SELF-ACCEPTANCE

D ID YOU KNOW THAT YOU CAN BECOME YOUR BEST SELF BY simply accepting your body appearance, your social worthiness, and achievements? Self-acceptance is a key ingredient to living a meaningful, successful, and happy life. Research shows that our intellectual ability does not have much to do with accepting oneself. The challenge one must take on is to come to term with oneself, as human being, regardless of our body appearance, social acceptance, and level of achievement. Accepting who you are is recognizing your nature (emotion and energy level), uniqueness (morality and rationality), and attitude (behavior), regardless of your walk of life.

Coming to terms with your human nature is about recognizing that you are not flawless, yet wonderful being. You can foster self-acceptance at any moment or stage of your life. You can do it, deliberately, using significant and meaningful events in your life. Accepting oneself can be inculcated, at any time in life and it be developed through events. Several traits such as social acceptance, body appearance, and self-confidence can hinder you from settling with your sense of self. Personality's traits such as narcissism and perfectionism are some personality's traits that can prevent from coming to terms with who you are.

Pure perfectionism can get our minds off the main things and cause us to sabotage small progress or underestimate our capabilities. The idea of self-acceptance can be understood, to some degree, from the concept of achievement. If achievement is tied to effort and aptitude, therefore, we can struggle to accept who we are or what we can do when we find ourselves unable to solve challenges or address obstacles we face.

SELF-ACCEPTANCE: A KEY INGREDIENT FOR LIFE SATISFACTION

A S WE TRANSITION FROM STAGES OF HUMAN DEVELOPMENT AND GROW older in life, we progressively face new and unfamiliar challenges. For example, during our early adulthood, most people are concerned about building family; developing lasting relationships, academic and professional goals as well as financial independence. Those various areas of life require time, energy, as well as cognitive, emotional, and psychological resources. One key ingredient in navigating through those challenges is accepting ourselves and having a nonjudgmental attitude toward each and all aspects of our life.

Warren Bennis, a research scholar and pioneer in the field of leadership, asserted that people should not be too concerned about becoming a leader; instead, they should be diligent in using all their human assets (time, energy, and knowledge) the best we can, without putting ourselves under unnecessary pressure. In other words, accepting what we have "going" and areas of improvement is a major sign of inner growth and healthy life. After all, self-acceptance is about coming to terms with things we like and things we hope to change in our life.

SELF-ACCEPTANCE: A KEY INGREDIENT FOR PERSONAL TRANSFORMATION

SELF-ACCEPTANCE IS A VITAL INGREDIENT TO TRANSFORM WHO WE ARE IS beyond what the naked eyes can see and dislike about us particularly when it comes to physical appearance, personality traits and qualities.

If you often feel embarrassed, uncomfortable with your physical appearance or you are only interested in accepting who you are when you are in shape, then there is a need to come to terms with your physical appearance, which includes our height, skin tone, and weight. You can come to terms with your body appearance by not comparing your appearance with that of someone else's.

It has become increasingly easy for us to overlook our human assets. Our daily life is filled with all kinds of advertisements and enticement that often become the reason for us to overlook and belittle our personal attributes. You can use your personality traits to develop and nurture your self-perception.

You can develop a solid self-view by recognizing some qualities that you show up in your day-to-day life. For example, if you tend to inspire or empowering other people in your everyday life, you can look at it as a gift to serve in the world around you. People's lives have purpose. When you do not contribute in the society you may feel excluded of the world around and become dysfunctional. Therefore, you should do your best to use your skills, gifts, and talents to meet people's needs. Taking on social role can also help to elevate ourselves and find meaning in our daily life. Grandparents, for instance, agree that parenting role can be rewarding and fulfilling.

DEVELOPING SELF-ACCEPTANCE

THE DEGREE TO WHICH WE ACCEPT WHO WE ARE IS USUALLY TIED TO HOW well we appreciate our physical appearance and hold ourselves from inside out. In other words, the extent to which we are happy is directly associated with physical appearance, social worthiness, and self-confidence. When you accept your physical appearance, you do not only project self-confidence, but you are also likely to protect and defend yourselves discrimination and the like. If you struggle to come to terms with yourselves, you might need to identify the specific area that robes away your self-acceptance. You should place an emphasis on that area in order to improve your level of self-acceptance. Experts warn about becoming too self-conscious in any of those areas, if we want to be happy and productive.

Physical acceptance can be described as our level of comfort and appreciation of our body despite not being completely pleased with all aspects of it. To enhance their physical appearance, many people spend huge amount of money on surgical procedures, amounting to $12 billion USD every year in the United States.

Social worthiness is about our emotional and psychological aptitude to defend ourselves in a social setting. With a low level of social worthiness, we tend to be afraid when other people evaluate us poorly; though we are in a social and casual setting, when we allow such feeling to take root in us, it can lead to state of social anxiety disorder, which is a severe condition of mental illness. It can be beneficial for you to adopt a nonjudgmental attitude toward yourselves, including others. The attitude of being at ease with self is likely to yield self-confidence.

In addition to the conventional understanding of self-confidence, this book also includes the premise that self-confidence is more about believing you can achieve whatever you set your mind onto. It is less about your abilities, skills, and knowledge, but your self-belief. Therefore, high self-confidence is having a favorable view of you, including your gifts and talents.

In summary, although healthy self-acceptance is an essential ingredient to developing a strong and rich identity, other negative feelings and thoughts can prevent many people from accepting who they are. Some of those feelings and thoughts include social anxiety, disagreeable self-values, and extreme perfectionism.

OVERCOMING OBSTACLES TO SELF-ACCEPTANCE

PERSONAL VALUES. IN TODAY'S ENVIRONMENT, PEOPLE TEND TO pay more attention to shortcomings than qualities. One way to develop a healthy brain is to acknowledge basic qualities, common to everyday people. You can build on common attributes to navigate this postmodern pressure. You are surely familiar with many them and probably already emulate some of them. Here are some of them

Attentive	Considerate	Organized
Adventurous	Constructive	Outgoing
Ambitious	Courageous	Peaceful
Aspiring	Hopeful	Perseverant
Athletic	Flexible	Persistent
Calm	Focused	Personable
Candid	Goal-oriented	Relaxed
Caring	God-fearing	Risk-taker
Charitable	Open-minded	Tolerant
Cheerful	Optimistic	Well-mannered

In addition to some of the qualities unique to you, start listing and accepting some of those attributes every day. You will be sure to developing a healthier view of you.

POSITIVE PERFECTIONISM. There is no debate that the pursuit of perfection has adverse consequences. Therefore, If pure perfectionism is an obstacle to self-acceptance, positive perfectionism can help to overcome obstacles and setbacks. However, it is important distinguish high standards from unrealistic expectations. High standards and unrealistic expectations. Some people have high standards than others and can be perceived as perfectionists. Critics of those with high standards may have that attitude for various reasons such as low self-confidence, poor self-image, or poor self-acceptance. Furthermore, we can be perfectionists when we are obsessed with details; extremely dedicated to work, impeding time for leisure; unwilling to be tolerant, when it comes to moral issues; reluctant to give up control; and extremely motivated and unable to control one own passion. People who do not feel loved enough and those who are unable to accept themselves may struggle with pure perfectionism. In short, poor self-acceptance can cause some people to seek perfection, even when it is not achievable, necessary, or warranted.

Positive perfectionism is a helpful way to develop nonjudgmental attitude toward who we are and what we do. For example, we can practice positive perfectionism when we choose to appreciate and value small progress, as opposed to looking at results in terms of success or failure. As Steve Jobs teaches, we cannot connect the dots looking forward, we can only do it looking afterwards. Consequently, we need to trust that things will fall in place when we look back.

Positive narcissism. Although the need to be loved and to love is a basic and fundamental ingredient to experience a meaningful and satisfied life, many people are more inclined to show love to others around them than toward their own selves. Many factors can prevent people from being kind and loving toward them. For example, a fast-paced life and some mistaken beliefs can prevent some people from developing a rich sense of self. One popular belief that prevents some people from developing self-acceptance trait is associated with narcissism. Narcissists are self-centered, egocentric, and careless about the welfare of other. Consequently, some people are unease about recognizing and celebrating their "blessings." In other words, many people are just afraid to be perceived as narcissists and end up discounting their talents, skills, and personality's traits. Nowadays, access to information is almost at the fingertips of anyone. However, information without perspective and context may have little impact on people's lives. For that reason, let us briefly go over the origin of narcissism.

According to Greek mythology, Narcissus was that young man who had seen a glimpse of his own reflection at a pond. He became so fond of himself and did not realize self-image is temporary. He also did not realize that the reflection of his image on the water was his outside appearance, as opposed to his inner self. As the mythology goes, unfortunately he died looking at himself.

There are several lessons about that story. First, we do not need to be so preoccupied about our physical appearance. Doing it can distract us from important matters in our daily life. Secondly, we need to "look good" outside and inside too. When we care for our inner self, we are likely to also care for our physical health and to maintain a healthy lifestyle.

Another possible lesson to be learned is that, we can distinguish negative narcissism and positive narcissism. Negative narcissism can be described as a focus on "Who am I?" as it relates to self-image and body appearance. We, as individual beings, have the same body's parts, head, arms, chest, legs, and so on. But people do not see themselves the same way. Some people wish they were taller, shorter, different skin complexion, or of different ethnicity and so on. We, as human beings have been fascinating living "creations." Therefore, we must be aware that self-image concerns can lead into self-destruction, self-deprecation, self-gratification, and irrational reasoning. In other words, negative narcissism is to be so centered and fascinated about oneself to the point of not caring about your true needs and those of other people around you.

In the contrary, positive narcissism can be described as to be appreciative of our beings (body and mind), who we are(identity), and to thrive to become what we can become(character, beliefs, values, and deeds). acknowledging the wonder of our creation and caring for external and inner needs and wants. Back to Greek mythology, Narcissus, the story indicates, because Narcissus was so fascinated by his beauty, one of his enemies made him believed to be admired by those who wanted him dead. Instead of negative narcissism, Narcissus could have used a positive lens of narcissism to develop his sense of integrity or character, get familiar with his core beliefs, and recognize what matter most in life, for him and people around.

In a broader standpoint, let us note that throughout history and across civilizations, stories, including fairy tales, have been used as a means of transferring valuable lessons. But one must analyze some of knowledge, beliefs, and values that have been transferred. Not be able to analyze our beliefs at one point in life might prevent us to life a more fulfill life. For example, the Greek mythology has prevented many artists from appreciating their own attributes for thousands of years, because perfectionism was only perceived through a negative lens. As a result, people have been reluctant to be innovators and trailblazers.

In today's social environment, some people struggle to be appreciative of their physical appearance and to make a fair assessment of their qualities. Valuable lessons can be learned from Narcissus' fable. Excessive self-admiration and self-centeredness can be harmful and destructive. However, not having an adequate sense of worth can be detrimental.

Today, experts from various fields underscore that low self-esteem and self-worth, feeling of rejection, and loneliness many people to succeed in their professions. In building strong relationships, and to live a happy life.

According to the American Psychiatric Association, here are some red flags when thriving to appreciative and becoming what we hope to become:

- Over self-representation
- Arrogance
- Overconfidence
- Tendency to overestimate
- Too sensitive to criticism and reaction

Recent study in social learning theory indicates self-admiration in itself is not a bad trait. It is described as an ingredient to be successful especially in today's socioeconomic environment, characterized by a fast-paced life, profound market transformation, increased uncertainty, and emerging social norms. For example, the easy access to advanced communication devices and platforms such as the social media is helpful for people to relate to the world around them. However, experts acknowledge that social media can be a platform for self-promotion and shallowness. In other words, many people feel lonely though not alone. Consequently, self-love, in addition to the genuine love of people (e.g., family, a few friends) closest to us, might be helpful ingredients to navigate the day-to-day disappointments, frustrations, and setbacks.

Inherently, we need a little of narcissistic traits in us to perform well under difficult situations, specifically when emotionally strength is needed. In fact, the groundbreaking research finding in social cognitive by the psychologist, Albert Bandura, has shown a direct relationship between *self-efficacy traits* and *narcissistic traits*. According to a study on social cognitive, qualities of self-efficacy include love, respect, wellness, self-empowerment, and personal accountability. There are, however, unequivocal differences between self-efficacy and narcissism. Being narcissistic is driven to impress people through self-image. Consequently, such person might display and irrational reasoning beliefs and might be highly visual due to his or her inability to reason logically. Narcissistic features are not encouraged; however, some of them can be used to lay ground for personal growth.

TAPPING ON YOUR GOOD NATURE

HEALTHY NUTRTITION IS IMPORTANT FOR NOT ONLY TO OUR BODY, BUT ALSO to our mental, emotional, and spiritual performance. When we fail to nurture the body, we found ourselves unable to be effective and productive. Similarly, when we fail to care for our mental, emotional, and spiritual needs, we are likely to feel exhausted, burnout, and unhappy. We do need to feed ourselves beyond the physical body to overcome the unenlightened side of us. Self-criticism, self-imposed fear, self-judgment, self-punishment, or inferiority and superiority complex are areas that we can only overcome through learning or some type of knowledge. Much can be learned from the Cherokee Indian mythology fable on making peace within self, which you are probably familiar with:

"A fight is going on inside me," grandpa said to his grandson.

"It is a terrible fight and it is between two wolves. One is evil—he is resentment, inferiority, anger, envy, sorrow, regret, greed, arrogance, self-pity, inferiority, lies, false pride, superiority, and ego."

The Cherokee man continued: "The other is good— he is truth, peace, serenity, love, kindness, humility, joy, kindness, hope, empathy, generosity, compassion, and belief. The same fight is going on inside you—and inside every other person, too."

The boy thought about it for a minute and then asked his grandpa, "Which wolf wins?"

The old man quietly replied, "The one I feed."

One basic step to become the best version of you is to nurture yourself in a holistic approach, which include your physical, spiritual, emotional, and intellectual sides. Sometimes, people find it difficult to be with themselves. Some people struggle to be alone because they do not have a healthy relationship with their own selves. Some people expect a lot from their own selves but fail to nurture and care of their selves. Psychoanalysis research indicates that people can have a master-slave type of personal relationship. Sometimes, people who might have that type of relationship with their own selves, they might also underestimate their own accomplishments as well as their personal strengths, skills, and qualities.

Some of the steps toward breaking away from a master-slave type of relationship is to recognize your human nature, which means to be tolerant with human flaws. Not making common human mistakes and errors a personal problem, or individual weakness. Next, not shying away from your qualities can also help nurturing a healthy relationship with self. Moreover, qualities come in hand in hand with preferences and styles. Be who are, do what you like and enjoy the most. Lastly, accept compliments from others. Take them as genuine. They are acknowledging the qualities. Do not see ourselves as those qualities, but simply a vessel of those qualities.

Let us remind ourselves that victories are products of our effort and inner strengths, which cannot be achieved through self-criticism, false pride, belittling, and self-deprecating. Genuine interest in personal growth is vital in becoming the best version of self. Growth is not a onetime event, but a way of life, which can be achieved through self-reflection.

PRACTICING SELF-AFFECTION

P EOPLE ARE OFTEN ASKED TO SHOW COMPASSION ABOUT OTHER PEOPLE'S life's predicament. But not many people, including children have been taught to love their selves. That social phenomenon has adverse consequences in people's lives. For example, in 2006, about 17% of college students reported to have been engaged in self-inflected injuries, based on a study conducted by Cornell and Princeton University researchers, one the largest studies on self-injurious behavior. According to experts, British and Canadians' college students face the same predicament.

People hold the belief that self-love is obvious to anyone. However, in early society, parents, guardians, and religious leaders did not stress on personal well-being and life happiness, as they are encouraged in today's environment. Ancient history shows that people essentially lived in a survival state of mind; ideas of personal well-being and wellness were absent. giving and sharing were practices to demonstrate love and affection. A regard for one's own well-being and happiness were not part of the everyday people, but that of kings, queens, and lords. The practice of self-love is a recent concept. Many people are still introduced and encourage to life a happy, by paying attention to their own needs and to stand for their own interests.

GIVING FROM A PLACE OF ABUNDANCE

T O CONCLUDE, TO SHOW LOVE TO OTHER PEOPLE AND TO ONESELF ARE NOT exclusive. In fact, Iyanla Vanzant, a spiritual coach and mentor, encourages people to give from a place of abundance and not from a place of lack. She explains that sharing from a place of lack is like making the receiving person a "thief." Self-love is not being selfish. It is about looking after one's own well-being and happiness. One safety instruction in the airplane, before take-off, specifies that parents and everyone else should first put on their own breathing mask before helping a child. This example shows that looking after one's own welfare is not necessarily about being a narcissist, as commonly perceived, but about placing oneself in the ablest position to help others. In the airplane's scenario, it is about minimizing causalities. Therefore, to be able to share with others, you must fully embrace who you are, love yourself, and desire the best out of your life.

A man is free when he sees himself for what he is and not as others define him.

—James Cone

Don't let the noise of others' opinions drown out your own inner voice.

—Steve Jobs

8

LIVING UNAPOLOGETICALLY

SOME CONCEPTS, LIKE UNAPOLOGETIC ARE POORLY UNDERSTOOD ACROSS cultures and people of various walks of life. There are relevant implications to that social phenomenon. For example, for many people the idea of being unapologetic means arrogant or self-important. But for trained minds, to be unapologetic, mean rejecting any kind of subjugation. Mohammad Ali, for example, was perceived as pretentious and audaciously proud of himself, particularly in the early years of his boxing career. For some people, to be unapologetic means boldness and the courage to refute any form of subjugation. It is repudiating the traps of social correctness and facing the inconvenient truth for the well-being of oneself and others. Moreover, to be unapologetic is to assert and elevate one sense of dignity and achievements. It is also recognizing that of other people. To be apologetic can carry regret, unhappiness, self-pity, a feeling of less than, or a not deserving attitude. Worse, to be apologetic can make you feel voiceless, although you might have your own opinions; or powerless and unenthusiastic, although you might have a purpose and passion.

Some people struggle to life unapologetically because they do not have a clear understanding on the subject. Other people struggle to be unapologetic because of their ill-upbringing. Becoming the best version of self requires coming to terms with who are and believing in what or who you aspire to. In other words, living unapologetically is not only asserting one beliefs and values, but it is also feeling secure and powerful enough to transcend any form of human subjugation.

If liberty is a birthright, freedom is not, but fought for. Everyone opinion matter if it is not ill-will. Therefore no one needs not to apology when there is not legitimate basis for it. One way to build up our unapologetic muscle is to not show empathy when it is not warranted. Some people have been brought up with the idea that showing respect to older people means not speaking up or not being assertive. Furthermore, in several societies around the world, not looking to an older person in the eyes while talking is perceived as a sign of respect. Unfortunately, it is nothing else but total subjugation and suppression.

According to some experts, it can be difficult for some people with ill-upbringing to alter their behavior, although they might hold leadership positions. Study indicates that it can be difficult to alter the behavior of people who have been subjugated in the name of politeness. Have you ever been asked not to express yourself as sign of respect or good manner? Many people have experienced that situation during their young age. When someone has not been encouraged to express himself or herself that person might not be able to be assertive enough later in life.

To conclude, in this postmodern age, human relation and social network has become increasing complex and absurd, therefore, in your journey to be your best self, it is essential you firmly assert and stand up for your opinions, beliefs, personal freedom and existential liberty.

LIBERTY AND FREEDOM ARE YOURS

MANY PEOPLE ACROSS THE GLOBE STRUGGLE TO BE UNAPOLOGETIC. Some people find themselves in that predicament because they feel unsecure, are not assertive enough to express their views, too self-conscious, or because they need constant approval. But liberty is a birthright, which means all men and women are created equal. Therefore, one way to become the best version of you is to recognize that you are not less than, but equal to, and a game-changer, designed to be on earth. Although, liberty is granted as basic rights to our humanness, personal freedom is not, as it is suggested in the literature on the subject. The literature of the subject also suggests that to earn your freedom, you must value who you are and others, and must stand against any forms of human subjugation. Nowadays, human oppression tends to be less physical, but rather mental, emotional, and psychological ensnarement. In a broad viewpoint, let us discuss liberty and freedom, as lived in various part of the world.

Concepts of *individualism* and *collectivism*, championed by Geert Hofstede, a psychology researcher, give a close look at how some advanced and developing societies experience liberty and freedom. Some of those societies are high in individualism (e.g., United States) and in collectivism (e.g., Japan); some societies are moderately individualistic (e.g., Germany, France, and Canada). Few are somewhat complex or a combination of the two dimensions (e.g., China, Brazil, and South Africa); though high in collectivism or individualism, those countries' economic systems are both capitalist and communist/socialist. That kind of layers complicate an attempt to develop a clear social understanding of liberty and freedom as experience in the day-to-day life of everyday people.

If people's way of life, including liberty and freedom go hand in hand, therefore, people's sense of liberty and freedom can be examined through the cultural lens of their respective societies. In other words, the level of clarity of the concepts of liberty and freedom in a society might have a direct consequence on the level of human rights, at the macro level. At the micro level, people's awareness of their humanity and sense of self as a direct implication on they function, interact, forge their personal identity, and shape the course of their lives.

If you are an avid follower of human rights news around the world, you are certainly aware of the complexity and absurdity related to liberty and freedom in some countries, as opposed to others.

However, in either type of cultural dimension, the real challenge for many people is to recognize the fine line between a person and a social being. There is no debate that people are social beings. However, our social traits are not what make us human, though being social is key ingredient to our ability to strive and thrive. Having a proper understanding of what makes you and other people human beings strengthens and enriches our sense of self, including your self-identity. But when our social needs and aspirations become the underlining criteria of what make us valuable, then self-actualization and self-realization become highly uncertain.

In a highly individualistic country, the socioeconomic environment prompts some people to define their sense of selves through personality traits. For example, in the United States, extroverted traits tend to be highly celebrated, as opposed to introverted traits. Consequently, many people favor extrovert qualities, including those who exhibit related traits. In the employment level, the sales industry is known to prefer extroverted employees though the sales job is a business transaction and a human experience. However, the sales organizations are known to have high rate of emotional exhaustion and burnout. This does not necessarily mean that other helping professionals, such as police officers, nurses, and social workers, face less pressure on the job, but that decision makers and experts in those related field (law enforcement; medical field) have an inclusive approach to what constitutes an effective and happy employee.

The key element is business leaders in the sales industry do not recognize that favorable emotional attributes are not limited to a particular personality type, but are present among extroverted and introverted employees. Consequently, sales employees must be equipped with professional competencies as well as human competencies, related to the job. Many educators understand that fact very well, based on their close interactions with students.

In countries high in collectivism, there is less emphasis on a person's emotion and energy level, but more on cognitive aptitude. You may be familiar with the mainstream debate over the Asian level vs. the American level of academic achievement and commitment to education. At the economic level, in high collectivistic societies, success requires being well-schooled, but at the social level, being well-educated is also being human. In societies, such as that of the United States, being successful at the economic level requires being smart, not really being well-schooled; being human is not much about being well-educated, but about being able to perform at a high level of vitality.

Based on those perspectives, the question is how you can develop a sense of personal human value. That question is important for at least two reasons. First although human value is self-evident, people are not usually educated on their human rights. Next, people's liberty and freedom are often infringed across nations, in daily basis. I share the belief that living unapologetically can help us uncover our humanness, as we see it fit, at the persona level. Lastly, personal liberty and freedom allow us to reject any form of subordination.

In conclusion, to be unapologetic is not about thinking more of ourselves, but instead acknowledging and embracing our human nature and condition, as well as living our individual life to its fullest. Liberty and freedom grow from within. They enable us to live the life we choose. They enable us to live free from self-imposed boundaries that do not benefit our well-being.

LIBERTY AND FREEDOM ARE NOT THE SAME

HUMAN BEINGS LEARN A LOT FROM NATURE AND THE WORLD AROUND ONE area in which human civilization has learned valuable lessons is through vegetation. People, like flowers develop and grow. Flowers grow and reach a point where they bloom fully. Although, plants stop growing at one point, people do not completely stop the growth process. People experience two types of development and growth: Physical growth (body) and inner growth (mind). Our invisible being or self also needs to grow to the point that, we, as human beings, can correctly express ourselves through our decision, behavior, and choices. Growth involves pain and affliction; overcoming pain and affliction is possible through personal effort and godly intervention. A quest for freedom

is one of the ingredients that make a godly intervention possible.

PROTECTING YOUR LIBERTY AND FREEDOM. Liberty and freedom intertwined in some level, but they are distinctive. Liberty can be defined as natural aptitude to be or to do without any self-evident restriction. In simple terms, liberty is freedom given to people by the nature. For example, when people, animals, or plants, come to live, they are already endowed with the aptitude to be and do in respect of their nature. They enjoy the gifts of nature. However, some people can deprive other people of their liberty. The absence of human dignity can also be perceived as being deprived of personal liberty. Slavery or Apartheid are some example of some people infringing on the liberty of others. Freedom can be defined as people's choice to assert their opinions, behaviors, and showcase their talents and skills. Generally, people's freedom can be infringed by anyone, including your neighbor, family member, or supervisor.

Although liberty is granted to humankind and freedom earned by people, history shows that, across human civilizations, liberty must be fought for, at least once in a lifetime, and freedom protected, almost all the time. For example, the well-recognized poet Chinua Achebe illustrates best how humility is perceived among some government officials in sub-Sahara Africa. For them humility is about thinking more of themselves and less of others:

> Worshipping a dictator is such a pain in the ass. It wouldn't be so bad if it was [sic] merely a matter of dancing upside down on your head. With

practice anyone could learn to do that. The real problem is having no way of knowing from one day to another, from one minute to the next, just what is up and what is down.

The misunderstanding of the idea of humility takes away its virtue, and such social phenomenon can be experienced in various social levels. Mike, for example, was born and raised in a land other than that of his biological parents. The social norms and beliefs in Mike's country of birth were more liberal than that of his parents. During his adolescent years, Mike's parents decided to return home, which uphold conservatism values and social norms, such as complete attitude of obedience in the name of respect to elders. Although, Mike recognized that those social norms and values were not self-empowering, but subjugating and self-deprecating, as well as weakening the soul and diminishing the character of individuals in the name of social and family hierarchy. After leaving his parents' home country, to countries with more liberal views, in his early young adult years, Mike recounted his struggle with mastering self-confidence and personal authority.

Even in most advanced societies, like the United States, the concept of humility has been misconstrued. For example, during the 2018 Winter Olympics in South Korea, the news outlets reported that the U.S. vice president and the top official of North Korea stood about 10 feet apart during the opening ceremony and did not greet one another. The two countries are known to be opponents for several decades. An article further indicated that the U.S. vice president did not want to be seen adopting Asian greeting manners, as the previous administration did. In fact, President Barack Obama was condemned by several news outlets during his official tour in the continent of Asia and even in Great Britain when visiting Queen Elizabeth. During those visits, Mr. Obama greeted his Asian counterparts using local norms, which include slightly bowing the head. He also did the same for the Queen. Although those official state visits included a welcoming handshake, the President was still criticized for bowing toward his counterparts. In the United States, humility is largely perceived as a personal weakness, being underprivileged, deprived, and having poor self-regard.

There is a general misunderstanding about the concept of humility for some reasons. The literature shows that because the concept did not receive a relevant degree of attention in the scholarly circle, it has been largely misconstrued. Fortunately, in recent years, research scholars have been concerned about the subject to improve people's lives at the personal and collective levels.

QUEST FOR TRUE KNOWLEDGE. Some people use the position of authority to achieve selfish interests. Unfortunately, many people easily fall prey to such practice and unethical behavior. History has shown stories that depict the desire of a few to rule over many through ungrounded truth. Periods of Enlightenment for example, in Greece, France, Germany, and in the United States highlight eras in which people rejected set of rules, practices, beliefs, norms, and customs that did not advance self-respect and basic human rights. But taking on those inaccurate beliefs and ideas came with great sacrifice. For example, history revealed that the man who stood against unfounded truth and beliefs was Socrates. He was so committed to knowledge based on truth that rulers of Athens voted for his death sentence, for being "a curious person, searching into things under the earth and above heaven." However, Socrates had already mentored many students; one of them was

Plato, whose intellectual prowess has also stood the test of time.

Throughout history, people have always been in a quest to subjugate fellow human beings. History also shows that it takes people from various walks of life to spread fresh ideas for the greater good of humankind. The idea of being unapologetic, for example, has been misconstrued. People have been distancing themselves from it, including its virtue. Consequently, millions of people across the world overlook the power of expressing their views and to live their life freely.

CORRECTING FALSE HUMILITY. Another step toward correcting our knowledge about the idea of humility is describing what it is not. Humility is not about being:

- Passive
- Dutiful
- Compliant
- Obedient

TRUE HUMILITY. In recent years, psychology scholars have shown a particular interest on the subject. According to a study, when properly understood, humility can be a valuable trait for empowering self, strengthening bonds, and encouraging social relationships, as reflected in the following examples:

Self-empowerment orientation

- Engaging in optimistic and healthy self-reflection
- Assessing oneself in terms of strengths, areas of improvement, and limitations
- Accepting acts of kindness without feeling embarrassed or belittled
- Restraining self and showing kindness

- Acknowledging compliments without being uncomfortable

Social relationship orientation

- Motivating self to work and reach achievements
- Avoiding being defensive or easily threatened
- Accepting awards and honor without being boastful
- Adapting to a team, group, and the environment
- Developing and enjoying quality social relationships
- Considering other people's rights and viewpoints

UNAPOLOGETIC FIGURES

ONE WAY NOT TO FEEL GUILTY ABOUT YOUR BLESSINGS IS TO acknowledge them. You do not have to shy away or feel embarrassed from the positive aspects of your life. Your accomplishments and good fortune contribute to your well-being. Shying away from your blessings can create a sort of mental and psychological distortion and malfunction, because you pretend to not be what you have become. If unfortunate events are also designed to build us up, so are fortunate events in life. Blessings should be taken for granted, or random events in life. They are meant to make healthy, not to create a sense of falsehood because we are afraid to be a source of inspiration. at ease with your blessings; affirm and enjoy them unapologetically. To living unapologetic takes character and a firm mindset. Let us now investigate the stories of two important people who have profoundly exemplified these characteristics over the course of their life: Condoleezza Rice and Mohammad Ali. While Rice exemplifies modesty in her unapologetic style, Ali's style of being unapologetic is without match.

CONDOLEEZZA RICE. In her book, *CONDI: The Condoleezza Rice Story*, Antonia Felix, revealed an unapologetic side of Dr. Rice, former United States Secretary of State under President George W. Bush, former policy advisor under President George H. Bush, and, university professor by training.

Dr. Rice asserted: "[I am] above average ... but not much more. When you've been a professor and provost at Stanford, you know what real genius is. I've seen genius, and I'm not it."

Although an appearance of humility was evident in her words, she did not shy away from recognizing who she has become. She has also been cognizant of the fact that several people looked up to her as a role model and leader in her communities. People who have followed politics during her tenure as the United States Secretary of State would validate what those who knew her said about her personality. With her high spirits, she was able to succeed in the field traditionally dominated by nonminority groups and earn the respect of people working inside the White House as well as the public.

MUHAMMAD ALI. Also known as the greatest, Muhammad Ali was one of the most respected and most admired sports people who ever lived. Formerly known as Cassius Clay, he was the African American who was born in an embryonic period of black consciousness and fought for social justice in the United States; he did not feel apologetic in any way about being a black person, a Muslim, and, most importantly, an American. In fact, one of the famous legal cases recorded in history, listing a defendant against the United States of America was that of Muhammad Ali. He brought the U.S. federal government to justice in the name of supreme consciousness. After four years of legal battle with the federal government, the U.S. Supreme Court unanimously overturned his conviction "for willful refusal to submit to induction into the Armed Forces."

In the world stage, Muhammad Ali earned his charisma mainly because, as someone said it well, "he had such a way with words." During numerous of his interviews and public statements, Ali could sound boastful, but unapologetic at the same time. For example, regarding his beliefs against being drafted for war, he stated:

> My conscience won't let me go shoot my brother, or some darker people, or some poor hungry people in the mud for big powerful America... And shoot them for what? They never called me nigger, they never lynched me, they didn't put no dogs on me, they didn't rob me of my nationality, rape and kill my mother and father.

Those words can be easily heard from controversial and inflammatory lenses. But trained minds can see past contentious views and appreciate the forceful and call for conscious behind those words. A New York Times eulogy article described him as "an agile mind, a buoyant personality, a brash self-confidence and an evolving set of personal convictions fostered a magnetism that the ring alone could not contain."

Muhammad Ali's unapologetic style is at the pinnacle because he was known as the most charismatic, captivating, and controversial sports figure of the 20th century who stood tall in turbulent times, and because he demonstrated he could be remembered as the greatest of all. The world has surely granted him that wish.

People are born equal, but different and unique. They personal experiences can make them exclusive, matchless, and inimitable. As Steve Jobs asserted, people do not have "to let the noise of others' opinions drown out [their] own inner voice.

To conclude, you can elevate yourself by having a clear knowledge about yourself, as a person and as a human being. You can also do it through your skills and talents. Both areas are unique traits designed to give you a voice and establish your social stature. Living unapologetically is not being arrogant or seeing oneself above other. It is affirming one presence and asserting oneself willingness to be, to be an active force, as opposed to only existing and making no impact in people's lives.

A man is free when he can determine the style of his existence in an absurd world.

—James Cone

It is up to each person to recognize his or her true preferences.

—Isabel Briggs Myers

9

BECOMING THROUGH YOUR PREDISPOSITIONS

HAVE YOU EVER MADE DECISIONS ON MATTERS OF IMPORTANCE BASED ON your styles and preferences and you have been disappointed? Well-known people from various walks of life have used their styles, even amid adversities.

EMBRACING YOUR PREDISPOSITIONS

IT IS BEYOND DEBATE THAT WE ARE DISTINCT HUMAN BEINGS. OUR predispositions and style what make us unique. Our style is meant to channel our energies, beliefs, and values in harmony and effortless. Our individual style is like a human signature. Most successful people have one, whether they are in Sports, Entertainment, Art, or Business sector. You ought not overlook your preferences or how you like to do what you do. It is your style; it is what make you unique and distinct. Your style encapsulates your predispositions. You can best channel your talents, knowledge, and beliefs through your style than otherwise.

Your preferences are made of several aspects of your life, such as family, childhood experiences, education, social class, personal exposure, employment history, professional exposure, and belief. Those elements are features or inputs of in your intellectual aptitude, acuteness and perceptiveness in any of your endeavor. Personal preferences are an important in leadership development. Embracing our personal preferences is not only a sign of self-assurance, but it also shows that you can assert what your need and want, particularly in matter important to you. You cannot be a free and happy person if you do not live up to your style. After all, knowledge, skills, and talents without style have little impact on people's lives. In other words, your style is a product of your predispositions or preferences. You can outperform yourself by tapping into your predispositions and preferences.

YOUR PREDISPOSITIONS ARE ASSETS

HAVE YOU EVER BEEN DISAVOWED AND INVALIDATED BY SOMEONE important to you, for being who you are and for emulating a quality that you perceived to be commendable? That was Robert's life story. Since his childhood, he had a distinct taste of life. He was a hardworking boy. As a young boy, he liked fine clothing, bakery, and European cuisine. He had a high regard on himself and life.

Robert's dad had an eye on him. He did not have much time to play and discover the world around with his peers in the neighborhood. However, he always managed to go to some fancy store for a treat. In fact, he probably discovered those places when riding with his dad. He had great taste and choice. He was not fond of traditional stable like his siblings. Shopping for clothing with him involved patience. He was not just going to get anything suggested by an adult person, including a salesperson. In fact, many people believed he was to some degree not an ordinary kid in his manner, including his ability to assume roles that were beyond his age.

Robert's mom somewhat reinforced his positive outlook of self and life. They had a healthy relationship. It is fair to say that he got some of taste and likes. She said nice things of him about the way he took care of himself. He took great care of himself, from quality clothes, clean bedroom to food. But, later in life, he realized that his mom had become in some ways cynical over his way of life. Her comments became sarcasms, though appearing as light jokes. and her remarks were judgmental, as opposed to protective. He did not know that some of the words his mom said to him quite often turned out to be his "demons", as he entered adult years living a life on his own. Later, Robert's cousin and close friend used her comments against him.

"You are full of yourself... you are boastful... you like to show off," were some of the words that Robert's mom often said to him, without instructing him how to behave. In Robert's mind, the opposite of being proud and boastful was extreme modesty. Subsequently, he drifted away from a healthy view of himself and life.

Robert did not experience the full impact of low self-esteem and self-worth when he was still around his family members and circle of friend. His poor self-view and low self-assurance came to light when he decided to leave his family and friends, in search for a better life. He travelled away from the care and security he knew, most of his life.

Robert's main problem was not so much about facing this external challenges and obstacles related to his new life in an entirely different environment, but much about reaching out to his inner abilities and potential, as well as standing up for his own welfare. His mom's words turned to be his main demons. For example, when he wanted to be self-confident and self-assured, he perceived himself to be arrogant. For many years, Robert struggled with low self-esteem and low self-worth, until he decided to live his life by pay attention to his personal values and preferences. Several years after living up to that decision he was able to find his voice and thrive for a better life.

USING YOUR PREDISPOSITION TO SUCCEED IN YOUR CAREER

HAVE YOU EVER FOUND YOURSELF STUCK IN A CAREER CHOICE, UNTIL YOU start acting on what you really believe in ? That was the case of Carl Rogers, an active Christian youth minister who, in his second year in theological college, began to realize that his personal predisposition might conflict with his career path; he decided to act on true beliefs. Rogers, now a renowned university professor and clinical psychologist, recounted that, though he was a remarkable student, deciding his career path based on his preference was a decisive aspect in finding his professional voice.

One way to uncover your unique qualities is to know your preferences and predisposition. Thus, you can showcase your uniqueness through your moral values and by asserting the basis of your line of reasoning. People's sense of humanity includes an individual opportunity to have a voice as well as to use and maximize their potential to the best of their abilities. By becoming aware of his core beliefs and line of reasoning, Rogers was able to forgo his initial career choice for one that aligned with his predispositions.

Several people from various walks of life have become who they are through their core beliefs and line of reasonings. Some of those well-known figures, now household names, include Microsoft founder Bill Gates Jr., the late Steve Jobs of Apple, the late former South African President Nelson Mandela, and former U.S. President Barack Obama. Mandela complied to be imprisoned for the values he cherished. After spending 27 years, he walked out of prison as a free man and became the first president elected in the post-apartheid South Africa. Obama declined high-paying job opportunities after completing his studies at Harvard University, where he became the first African American ever to be president of the Harvard Law Review. (Peter Yu was Obama's predecessor as president of the Harvard Law Review. After graduation, Yu served as a clerk for Chief Judge Patricia Wald at the U.S. Court of Appeals for the Federal Circuit.) Obama instead went on to be a community organizer in the South Side of Chicago, a dysfunctional landscape of poor neighborhoods in the city. The rest is history. His beliefs had enabled him to stay the course of life, which led him to become the first African American president of the United States.

In summary, our predispositions and our core beliefs are meant to help become the best of ourselves. You too can live your own life based on what you like and value the most.

PART 4

IDENTITY CLARITY IN A HOST COUNTRY

Not all those who wander are lost.

—J. R. R. Tolkien, *The Fellowship of the Ring*

We have always believed it possible for men and women who start at the bottom to rise as far as the talent and energy allow. Neither race nor place of birth should affect their chances.

—Robert F. Kennedy

10

THE ADVENTURER PERSONALITY

O NE MAJOR ASPECT OF LEAVING HOME IS TO BECOME THE BEST WE CAN be. It is an opportunity for you to discover the way of life in other countries, which can be experienced through religious beliefs and social practices, socioeconomic behavior, and political rhetoric. Therefore, it is essential to be aware of that dynamic for you to be critical, as you go about becoming the best version of you, including success in various aspects of life.

When it comes to developing a clear sense of self through lived experiences, some academic researchers and those who choose to live in a foreign land have one thing in common: They put on various "hats" or go through experiences that nurture and strengthen their sense of selves. I learned it from my own life experiences, as someone who ventured in other part of the world, and as a junior researcher.

As doctorate student, I had been extensively involved in research, including reading and writing, which I had not been used to, prior to reaching that stage of my academic journey. Research is typically about exploring and examining a specific subject or area of study with uncertain outcomes, although assumptions can be made based on existing knowledge. Researchers, like people who venture in other part of the world, engage in unfamiliar territories. While researchers learn from reading and thinking, those who migrate get new knowledge by interacting with local people

During my academic journey, I read materials beyond my major. Constructive feedback from instructors encouraged that attitude. So, I was enthusiastic about reading articles from various disciplines (e.g., philosophy, anthropology, psychology, or sociology), though I was enrolled in management program. I was particularly interested in reading materials outside of my major because I experienced meaningful development and growth in the process. It was like getting food for the soul and human spirit. Moreover, extensive research in various disciplines is helpful in developing aspects of the intellect (mental, emotional, and psychological). These aspects of being engaged in academic activity influence the students' personal and academic viewpoints because learning is also a *hermeneutic of lived experience*. Specifically, students are consciously engaged in making sense of the knowledge content through their individual background. Thus, they are likely to gain an in-depth understanding of the same learning material, including concepts and theories.

To some extent, the lived experiences of academic researchers and people who adventure in different part of the world have some things in common. Before we take a close look at some of the similarities, let us start to describe the term *adventurer* and highlight some of its typical features. Adventurers can be described as those who are excited about exploring unfamiliar locations, though the trip may be somewhat perilous and involved unfamiliar places. They are aware that the outcome of the experience includes a degree of uncertainty, despite having gathered enough information related to the road ahead. The probability to succeed is largely tied to their ability to think, plan, reason, and communicate effectively.

An adventure and a scholarly research initiative are closely related. Individuals involved in these endeavors explore unfamiliar terrain, feel excited about the initiative, reach a level of uncertainty, and demonstrate the right skills and attitude in the course of accomplishing the goal. However, people go adventure in other part of the world can learn from those form an opinion through a systematic approach of handling data, just as those involve in academic study.

For example, effective and successful researchers should understand their position as investigators, think systematically, and behave appropriately. As a result of being fair-minded, researchers are not likely to succeed in the professional endeavor, but also to transform their personal life, even when their professional aptitude seems inappropriate to assume their role.

The real-life story of Brené Brown, a research professor, can be the best illustration of such occurrence. She recounted, in her TED talk, that she experienced a personal breakdown while researching on why some people show courage and others do not. One of the groundbreaking findings was that those who are courageous are the ones who can function well from a position of vulnerability. That self-awareness led her into a personal crisis, which lasted for about five years. Today, she is the voice of authority on vulnerability.

She was involved in that research with a clear understanding of her role. Although she laid aside her biases, views, and personal aspirations while undertaking that initiative, she ended being deeply influenced and transformed in her personal and professional life through the overall experience. That research study became an opportunity to develop a stronger and richer self-identity.

Likewise, people who go into unfamiliar geographic locations, just like going to another county, can also grow inside out; however, they become involved in overcoming various challenges and obstacles, which include having to deal with incidents associated with their social identities as spy, tourist, prisoner, and missionary. Usually, people who go into new and unfamiliar places get excited and enthusiastic about the idea of traveling. However, those who are effective and successful are those who can behave beyond their social identities.

People, including the millions of immigrants, who go for an adventure into an unfamiliar environment, are prone to face the challenges and obstacles involved in their social identities, primarily because they are not settlers. They must adapt and integrate to the socioeconomic tapestry of their environment. Therefore, self-actualization (becoming the best self) and self-realization (achieving full potential) for millions of immigrants in the United States and around the globe do not only depend on aptitude to transcend personal biases, prejudices, cynicism, including negative criticism, and illusionism, but most importantly, they are closely tied to their aptitude to develop a strong, rich self-identity.

People involved in research and those who adventure in another part of the world are afforded an opportunity to strengthen their sense of selves in ways that can change their beliefs values, and dreams. In short, people in both groups to succeed in their experiences need to develop and nurture a strong and rich sense of self.

SPY'S FEATURE

I N THE 1600s, THE FIRST EUROPEANS WHO MIGRATED TO NORTH AMERICA had no intention to return to their homeland. For them, it was a one-way trip. As indicated in history, they wanted to escape from religious and political tyrannies. They went to North America to settle there, without any form of loyalty to their home countries. People who first migrated to the United States are commonly referred to as *settlers*. Their migration experience was unique and unconventional. Most people who migrated to a host country still hold a form of loyalty or attachment to their homeland, though they may have left to save their own lives or the lives of their families. Therefore, it is common for many immigrants to experience conflicting feelings about where their "true home" is. They face an unconscious dilemma, which may hinder them not to be completely committed to a host country. They experience a conflict of loyalty, which is another trait or feature of the adventurer.

As immigrant to the United States or elsewhere, you too might have that kind of experience. You might say to yourself, "I do not need to buy a decent vehicle or a house," because you are thinking about returning home in a distant future. You live in a new home country but feel the United States while being homesick, though you do not see yourself readapting to the everyday life of your country of origin. Consequently, you become uncertain about whether to settle in the United States or return to your homeland. Your inability to settle can make you feel unsecured about the prospect of living a successful life. You have probably become suspicious about your way of life; you do not seize or pursue life's opportunities; or you sabotage your effort to live the life you want. Overcoming an unsettled and undecided mindset require baby steps toward openness, flexibility, and vulnerability.

TOURIST'S FEATURE

A S AN IMMIGRANT ARRIVING TO THE UNITED STATES, you face the possibility to behave and see life through the eyes of a tourist. For example, if you live in major touristic cities like Washington, D.C., Las Vegas, or Manhattan, you have surely noticed that what almost everyone visits are famous places, such as the White House, Capitol Hill, or Times Square, creating memories by taking at least a dozen pictures. Visitors may have thought, "I am here," or "I am also here," "I was there," or "I was also there," while taking those pictures. It is somewhat a sense of realization or desire to gather evidence that shows personal and social accomplishments. You probably have done that yourself when you first arrived in the United States. I remembered visiting some of those places and a friend was taking picture of her first snow season ever.

Some people taking pictures come from outside the United States and just visit a relative for a short time. They are tourists in the true sense of the word. Maybe you are a U.S. citizen and have been a U.S. resident for many years; there may be a tourist identity in you, though you might not be fully aware of it. There are favorable and unfavorable aspects in social phenomenon.

NEGATIVE MINDSET. Some people are likely to experience the tourist identity when they face problems and obstacles. They contemplate about giving up on their dreams or giving in to themselves. To get a sense of comfort, some might think, at least, "I was here" and visited this country, seen as the "paradise" on earth, though feeling distressed in the Land of Opportunity. I see it as an undesirable mindset of the tourist inherent in the adventure, away from the country of origin.

The attitude of tourism begins to take place in your mind when you first had the idea of coming to the United States. It happens without you being aware of it. For example, before the age of the Internet, many immigrants had an idea about life in the United States, mainly through TV shows (soap opera, comedy series, among others) and movies. Since the advent of the Internet, the world has truly become a global village and many people around the world who want to come to the United States can dream day and night about their new life in the Land of Opportunity. Some are eager to visit well-known places, meet celebrities, and take selfies to capture some of those experiences. Although such daydreaming can be a source of anticipation toward accomplishing an important goal, such cannot leave you with a wandering mind and an adventuristic attitude.

A tourist attitude can grow and manifest itself among immigrants when overwhelmed by the day-to-day routine and problems inherent in the Land of the Free. Other than the early European migrants who first came to this land, in 1920, through a ship called Mayflower and those brought from Africa through slavery, the majority of people who migrated to the United States had Plan B: return to their home countries or go somewhere else (e.g., Canada). In other words, almost everyone who migrates to the United States is susceptible to have the tourism syndrome, which might hinder self-determination.

Those who come to the United States for education are likely to struggle with the tourist syndrome for several reasons. First, they may be tempted to visit and discover many places as they possibly can because of the idea that of returning home at the academic goals. Plan B is to return home after completing education. If they are not careful enough, such line of reasoning can detract their main goals. Many foreign students choose to stay after graduation due to the high standard of life and the economic opportunities that the United States offer. Some of them might not, unconsciously, fully integrate in the social fabric of their new home country, until they completely come to terms that they have made the United Sates their new home. As immigrant, it necessary to follow the footstep of those Europeans who first to the U.S: They made the conscious decision to settle, which enable them to conquer and prosper in that side of the globe. Next, summertime is generally perceived as a period of relaxation and vacation in the United States and countries with similar seasons. Some people might only use that time for such purpose and lose sight of matters important for them, including making sense of life, in general. Though, summertime is the most preferred time of the year for indulgence, it is important to be mindful of matters of importance to oneself and life.

In summary, people face the challenge of nature versus nurture, therefore it is necessary for immigrants to stay committed to the main reason in the U.S and also nurture their sense of selves, in order to life a successful and meaningful life.

POSITIVE MINDSET. The idea of tourism is mainly about visiting new and unfamiliar places. It is about going to places that lift the spirit, nurture the soul, strengthen the heart, and free up the mind. People who usually have a fulfilling vacation experience some of those aspects. Usually, people who pursue their hopes, goals, and dreams away from home are somewhat aware of those aspects. But those who succeed and get satisfactory outcome are those who hold firmly on some of them. Immigrants can tap on those features to not give up on their dreams while giving in to their sense of ingenuity and maximizing their potential.

Positive tourist identity is about being cognizant of the pros and cons of going to unfamiliar places and adjusting to a satisfying life. Those who demonstrate such characteristics are those who can stay inquisitive in the new environment. They understand that learning is a lifelong journey and they remain teachable to grow and improve. They understand there is a time for everything—to work, study, play, rest, or have fun.

Betty, a young lady who migrated to the United States from Africa, exemplifies those traits; she is a grad student at one of the universities in the state of Maryland. She made a point to go out every other week, even for a walk in the mall. She explains that it gives her an opportunity to relax and reenergize for the milestone ahead. To the surprise of some of her friends, she has been able to hold on to that lifestyle since she started her undergrad program; she is now a grad student. The ability to live a balanced lifestyle can be challenging, but difficult to achieve when you are blindsided by its favorable impact on your overall level of productivity, ingenuity, and life satisfaction.

Rose is also a grad student, but she finds it difficult to take the time to rest and have fun. She mainly spends most of her time between school, religious activities, and helping acquaintances. She explains that her strenuous schedule does not allow her to find time for self-care, though she admits her inability to say no to demands and requests she cannot meet.

Tourists are generally described as people who go to unknown places; nurture their creative mind and spirits; and live an unconventional life. In the United States, Nigerians are particularly known as the most dynamic.

The tourist's side in an adventurer has significant adverse consequences, when poorly handled. Sometimes, tourists fall in love with the visiting place and experience mixed feelings about whether they want to stay or return to their home country. That uneasy feeling can also affect your ability to do well in the areas of your life and grow as a person—academically, professionally, or socially, until you make it clear to yourself about your goals. Mixed feelings can make you become indecisive about how you live your life, including your day-to-day routine and interaction with others. When visiting places, people take pictures so that they might show and remember where they have been. They can say, "I was there" or "I was also there." Similarly, as immigrant, you should be careful about living with "I was also there" mindset. Such mindset can keep you to grow and transform your life. Simply put, the touristic effect can cause someone to discount life's given opportunities. But when you recognize it, an effectively integrated life can be an essential ingredient to achieving your goals and living a successful and meaningful life in your new home country.

PRISONER'S FEATURE

MANY F IMMIGRANTS FEEL LIKE THEY ARE STUCK IN one part of the world despite of their abilities and freedom to travel outside the United States, for various reasons. For example, many of them have been living in the U.S for so long that it has become difficult for them to return to their motherland. The cost of visiting their homeland and taking off from work are factors that can prevent many immigrants to maintain and develop ties with family members, relatives, and friends. In addition, it is common for people who live in developed societies such as the United States to feel like life for them has just begun a routine with no opportunity to engage in meaningful and fulfilling activities, at the personal and professional levels. Such feeling can leave many people in a state of boredom and, eventually feeling prisoner within their own self. For immigrants, the feeling of being a prisoner can also be experienced because they are unable to a life they hoped for. One way to be free from such feeling is to take the journey of self-discovery, which can be achieved through soul-searching, self-reflection, and meaningful interactions.

MISSIONARY'S FEATURE

MANY PEOPLE WHO COME TO THE UNITED STATES ARE GENERALLY pleased to be in a country where they are encouraged to be sensitive to people's pain and suffering. The United States is well known to be one of the most charitable countries in the world. That attitude is somehow contagious. Consequently, many people who arrived in the United States also tend to concern themselves with matters they genuinely care about but get involved too early or without the appropriate knowledge or understanding of their new environment. As a result, some people mismanage their time, energy, finances, and other possessions. They get sidetracked from their main goals, dreams, and aspirations.

The United States is home to many religious beliefs. Some of them are known to prey upon millions of people who have newly arrived in the country. Whether you have been living in the United States for many years or have just come to the U.S and you are interested in being fair-minded and developing a strong and rich sense of self, you should be careful about unfamiliar religious and spiritual congregations with beliefs and practices that radical from everyday life. While some of them are not difficult to recognize, others can be difficult to recognize because they are well-structured and organized. There is a consensus that Jehovah Witness and The Church of Jesus Christ of Latter-day Saints, informally known as Mormon Church, best exemplified well-structured and organized religious organizations. Those religious organizations tend to abide by the letter of the law and overlook the spirit of the spirit. Furthermore, in the name of a religious renewal movement within Protestant Christianity, many faith leaders have been selling the idea of a direct experience of God. The quest for a personal experience of God with have been the main cause for radical and extremes religious belief and spiritual practices in the

United States of America and around the world. Several examples of them are well-documented.

Jonestown massacre, for example, is one of those tragic occurrences ever recorded in the U.S. history, in the name of religiosity. James Warren Jones, alias Jim Jones, was an "idealist and loving people"; he was an American religious leader who managed to gather 900 of his followers in the jungles of Guyana, in November 1978. Jones encouraged them to protest about the inhumane conditions of people in the world, by drinking poisoned Kool-Aid. According to a New York Times article, Jim Jones was "a trained Pentecostal minister ... with polished oratorical skills."

Another case of extreme religious practice happened in Middlesboro, Kentucky. According to an article by ABC News, Jamie Coots, the pastor of the Full Gospel Tabernacle in Jesus Name, handled a snake and got bitten during a religious service. The pastor died later when he arrived home. Before leaving church, he rejected any treatment in the name of God. Study indicates that the use of snakes in places of prayer is a century-old practice in the United States. Recent surveys showed that about 125 churches are involved in similar practice.

If you are not careful enough when you get to an unfamiliar country such as the United States, you can jeopardize not only the main reason of your trip, and aspirations, but you might also stray away from your best self. Nevertheless, life around and the challenges you face can build you up, transform you into your best self, or turn you into someone you would not want to become. Your missionary side can be a helpful ingredient in your identity development, when properly considered.

FACING YOUR DISCOMFORT

IN THE UNITED STATES, JUST LIKE ANYWHERE ELSE IMMIGRANTS TEND TO STAY together and thrive to maintain a bond and a sense of one accord. Although a support system can be essential to strive and thrive in a host country, relying largely on people of similar cultural heritage can hinder you from becoming your true self and from attaining a more fulfilling life.

Study in sociology shows that it is common for some members of a group to make poor decisions because they have been influenced by other group members. Such social phenomenon is referred to as *groupthink*, a term coined by Irvin Janis, a social psychologist. Groupthink has adverse effect on people's ability to think and think critically by themselves and for their welfare. Groupthink can keep you from having your own opinion based on your personal experience. Moreover, it can also have an adverse effect on your moral, ethical and intrapersonal competency.

Janis, one of the pioneers of the concept highlighted its effect among a group of people as follows:

- Illusion of invulnerability
- Tendency to moralize
- Feeling of unanimity
- Pressure to conform
- Opposing ideas dismissed

The concept of groupthink has been identified as the main cause of several major poor decisions among high level government officials of the United States. For example, political experts converged that the Bay of Pig invasion or the Japanese attack on Pearl Harbor happened mainly because government officials, including President J.F.K were under the effect of the groupthink. Political experts asserted that at some levels of the U.S. Army officials, members of the team placed group harmony over critical thinking

Regardless of their origin, ethnicity, or gender, people become a group when they come together. Based on my personal experience and research on the subject of groupthink, it is common for the ordinary person who comes to the United States to get a groupthink experience in some areas of his life, to some extent. As an immigrant though, it can be comfortable to build your life around those with similar cultural heritage. You do not only face the probability to have the same level of thinking you had before you arrived in the United States, but you might also make the same mistake as your peers. Consequently, you may impede your process of human development and growth, as well as cultivating a strong and rich self-identity.

Human beings are social beings; we are directly and implicitly members of a community, whatever kind of groups it may be. Everyone must belong to a community to live a balanced life. Therefore, it is essential that you thrive to use various lenses and think outside the conventional norms to think critically. Failing to do think critically can prevent from getting the result you want.

To put it altogether, embarking onto an adventure is a multifaceted phenomenon. It is beyond debate that life in the United States is difficult and challenging. Those who choose to come to the Home of the Brave can easily get distracted, face unpredictable events, and deal with unexpected conditions. But leaving your homeland is like getting out of your comfort zone. Leaving your home country does not have to be a one-way trip. Making your host country your home does not mean forgetting your place of origin, your cultural heritage, and, most importantly, your personal story—the big picture. It is can be an opportunity for self-realization, self-actualizations, and life transformation.

Destiny is no matter of chance. It is a matter of choice. It is not a thing to be waited for; it is [not] a thing to be achieved. [Destiny is a state of being, a place called NOW].

—William Jennings Bryan

Your life is your life.

—Charles Bukowski

11

YOUR AMERICAN DREAM

NON-U.S. BORN USUALLY LEAVE THEIR HOME COUNTRY AND PEOPLE THEY dearly love for a worthy cause. They surely do it in the pursuit of their dreams and goals. In fact, the biblical scripture teaches that God led his people in new land and places to live a life full of "milk and honey", a life beyond dreams and imaginations. You too have left your home country for a new place, a new land, a place where you can have a life beyond your wildest dreams and imagination.

After all, there is no better reason to leave a place of comfort to become a best version of oneself and reach peak point in life.

Away from your homeland, you can become aware of matters that are important in your life. You can reach a place of destiny or existential calling. But it may not happen without a strong and rich sense of self, which is a crucial element for maximizing your potential and becoming the best self and live a fulfilled life.

BEING ENTHUSIATIC AND CREATIVE

T HE MOVIE, FROST/NIXON BASED ON A TRUE STORY ABOUT THE 1972 Watergate's scandal under President Nixon who subsequently resigned as the President of U.S, two years after the scandal, is also the story of someone who was determined to live his "American Dream." David Frost, in real life, was a TV show host whose subject of interest had nothing to do with politics. However, to increase his professional influence, he planned to interview Nixon and the plan materialized. Frost's goal was to have Nixon admit his involvement in the Watergate scandal to the American public and the world. That was a tall order for several reasons. Nixon had consistently denied that accusation and chose to resign from the office rather than having to explain himself before the justice system and the TV screen. In addition, no journalist had been able to make such attempt. Interestingly, Frost had no previous experience in politics and was not even an American or a resident of the United States. In that movie, Frost was asked why he was determined in pursuing such adventure to the point of contracting debt to finance the project, including Nixon's fees. Frost replied, "Success in America is not like success anywhere else."

As you probably know, Frost instigated Nixon to confess what he had not previously done, in front of the American people through television broadcast. To the disappointment of Nixon's staff and himself, Frost was able to break through the emotional and psychological mechanism preset for that interview. You can say Frost's professional and personal life went to the "roof" while that of Nixon landed the lowest level after the interview.

The movie can be informative and inspirational for those who choose to make the United States their new home. First, America is the Land of Opportunity for millions of people around the globe. Americans refer to their country as the Land of Immigrants to acknowledge the early Europeans who migrated to that side of the globe, to free themselves from religious persecutions and authoritarian regimes. Even nowadays, America is still regarded as such. A beacon of hope, regardless of people's aspirations, includes education, employment, professional training, business, political influences, entrepreneurship, religious practice, and unconventional social norms, among other factors to be able to sustain oneself in a foreign land.

YOUR HEART AND BRAIN ARE CONNECTED

JUST LIKE DAVID FROST MANY PEOPLE AROUND THE WORLD FORTUNES TO go to the United States. But some people who have managed to make it in there, let their goals and dreams slip away for one reason or another. Those who have been able to achieve their dreams and goals have not only be able to adapt in the environment, but they have also been to listen to their heart and seize potential opportunities.

Did you know that your heart and brain are the first parts of your human body that begins to take form at the germinal level? In other words, while you were in a fetus form in your mother's womb, your heart and brain were the first parts to develop. The life in you begins to manifest itself in your heart and brain through your blood and neuronal system. So, you would not aspire to become what it is not naturally possible or what you are not capable of accomplishing, because your makeup is organically predisposed to fulfil those aspirations in life, within your environment and the world around you.

It is for crucial for you to address matters that are important for a rewarding and meaningful life. Your personal and professional goals and aspirations are part of matters that should concern you the most, because they come from your heart and brain. Therefore, it's vital that to make sure they aligned, not only with your values and, but important to predispositions or preferences. Life important goals and aspirations are not only embedded in our characters and predispositions, but they also flow from our heart and brain.

Like David Frost, you can reach the next level in personal and professional life in away from home if you focus in important matters in life and to you.   It is a waste for you and your true self not to go after matters that are important to you (e.g., your life ambitions, hopes), because you are simply busy and live to work. The life in you can manifest itself if you follow your heart, your aspirations, and your dreams.

FACING YOUR DISCOMFORT

TYPICALLY, EVERY MAJOR CHALLENGE OR PROBLEM HAS MENTAL, emotional, and psychological component. When you are facing a problem, you might not be able to accurately predict how it will unfold, as you seek to address it. But you reflect on the mental, emotional, and psychological aspects of the problem, to capture the practical and abstract elements of the challenges, as well as recognize the necessary resources to stay the course and get the outcome you want. As a U.S.

immigrant, you evidently need more emotional and psychological capital to succeed in a highly hyper and sophisticated social environment, such as the United States.

ADAPTING TO NEW SOCIAL NORMS. Now that you are in the United States, it is essential for you to grow inside out because, otherwise, your life goals and aspirations might slip away; in addition, you might miss the opportunity to live a happy and satisfied life. One sure way to grow inside out is by adapting new social norms, as opposed to simply using them to get by. For example, some people speak English enough to run errands and appear acculturated, which can prevent them from becoming the best version of them. A rich and strong life include the ability to communicate our views and thoughts, our feelings, and our perception, especially when it comes to matters most important to us. Another way to adapt to new social norms in the U.S is to critically about those unfamiliar social norms and embrace them as you see appropriate

To *adapt to* means having the ability to express or speak freely from a position of wholeness, rather than a position in which you feel unable to correctly and fluently express your views from your heart and soul, due to poor verbal skills, or perhaps, you lack the proper social and behavioral norms. Although the U.S. population is a melting pot society, its social learning rate is high compared to other nations in similar ranking. In other words, though you may come across people of similar ethnicities, they are likely to interact with you through the country's social norms. It can be more beneficial for you to go beyond the ability to speak, but also to adopt the country's social norms.

For a non-U.S. born American, failing to effectively integrate American social and behavioral norms can be a major barrier to pursue a personal dream and aspiration. As a social being, your growth and well-being are tied to the environment in which you live, work, and play. If you choose to not integrate in the way of life in America, based on the American perspective, not based on yours or that of your community as a whole, then you might not be able to grow as a person and pursue your dreams and aspirations. You need to leave your social and behavioral comfort zone and embrace those of your host country that fit your style, preference, and aspirations. Living within your social and behavioral comfort zone keeps you from maximizing your potential.

In a host country, you are in new and different environment, a place you must adapt to, without losing sight of your preferences, qualities, and gifts. You might to go through pain, disappointment, frustration, or rejection, for whatever reasons. You may now not see the need of immersing yourself in the social fabric of your host country but consider this: Psychology experts encourage people to not make unwanted situations and outcomes personal; otherwise, they might develop a victim mindset, which you do not want.

DRAWING A BIGGER PICTURE. If you are an immigrant, chances are you were not raised in a purely individualistic environment. America's individualistic society is at top of that group. So, even though many developed economies and western nations have an individualistic culture, which of the United States is truly dominant. In an individualistic country, the pace of life is fast, people are assertive, proactive, and self-reliant. People who come from a collectivistic society, such as Brazil, China, and many countries in Africa, the pace of life is slow, or not as fast as that of an individualistic country, people tends to follow collective norms, and handle uncertainty poorly. Although people who come to live in the United States face the challenge of adapting to the environment, they also need to adopt its social and behavioral patterns. To function well and live a satisfied life, it is important to recognize that those who come from a collectivistic society must uncover social and behavioral norms of their homeland that fundamentally differ from that of individualistic societies, like the United States of America.

Research shows that many people who have chosen to make the United States their new home may still struggle to adopt to Western societies in a way they achieve their goals and aspirations. Although part of the reasons is due to be unfamiliar with the dynamics of life in individualistic society, but part of it is also tied to previous way of life and upbringing of those who migrate.

BECOMING THROUGH SOCIAL NETWORKING. As a migrant in the United States, just like anywhere else, you are likely to form and build your first relationship among people from your country or with other immigrants. The caveat is that you may fall into group thinking and live the lifestyle of people in your community. If you had goals and aspirations, you might be able to achieve them, but if you do not, you might not be able to maximize your full potential. The reason for this is that to fulfill your goals and aspirations in a host country, you essentially have to connect with people of your country or other immigrants; you also need to immerse yourself in the fabric of the society in which you live, work, and play.

OVERCOMING CONFLICTING SOCIAL NORMS. If you are a working professional or businessperson and are not originally from a traditionally individualistic country such as the United

States, then you may struggle to assert your individual leadership or authority in your day-to-day professional life. National cultures that are not individualistic lack opportunities in which leader qualities are instilled on citizens. Subsequently, it is probable you had little to no exposure to leader traits during your upbringing and in your social life. Beliefs do not usually operate in the conscious mind, but in the subconscious. Therefore, although you may have an idea of what your beliefs are in your conscious mind, much of what you believe is in your subconscious.

By default, we use of our conscious mind to perform professional tasks and assume professional roles. Therefore, when functioning in different environment our subconscious can interfere with the conscious mind. Most people experience such dynamic when learning another language. One should be aware that dynamic and educate the subconscious mind about the new environment. Customs and social norms, which you first learned and embraced, can still hinder your development and growth, if you do not take the time to uncover and recognize them. You may have gained some workplace values, as well as social and behavioral norms from your formal education and training; however, significant professional growth and success require a significant inner growth and transformation.

You can empower yourself by first being aware of your inner conflicts between the social norms and behaviors you first learned during your childhood and teenage years, as well as those of your host country. Next, you can enthusiastically choose to integrate social and behavioral norms that fit your aspirations and the environment in which you live, work, and play.

Essential social norms for interpersonal communication skills include:

- Firm handshake
- Eye contact
- Proper proximity
- Not interrupting the speaker
- Active listening
- Being assertive

USING YOUR PERSONAL AUTHORITY. You can develop your personal authority and self-respect by acknowledging and embracing your personal heritage. You can also do it by helping people to acknowledge your personal heritage, which can be defined as "something that comes to [someone] by reason of birth." No human should be ashamed of who he or she is, including his or her heritage.

Study reveals that first- and second-generation immigrants tend to undervalue, and drift away from, their cultural heritage; however, the fourth-generation immigrants tend to claim their national heritage. One of the reasons the first and second generations are inclined to overlook their cultural heritage is that they tend to be so preoccupied to adapt and succeed at the expense of their cultural identity. Those who value their cultural heritage are not only likely to adapt effectively, but they succeed and live a satisfied life. Utah's Mia Love, for example, is a second-generation immigrant; she is the first black female Republican and the first Haitian American elected to Congress.

The point is that you can use your heritage to exercise your human authority and sense of self in your workplace, community, and school. In your workplace, for example, you may not have a positional authority, but you can use your personal authority to earn respect and self-respect. Positional authority is that power which comes with the job title, while self-respect and is that power which comes from who you are as a person and as a human being. It is a basic human right to be respected, to pursue your personal aspirations, and to live a fulfilled life, irrespective of your national heritage. Lastly, you can also assert your authority through your professional expertise. In the United States, more than elsewhere, expert knowledge is a sure way to earn respect in the workplace environment.

THE POWER OF PERSONAL INTEGRATION. On one hand, the U.S. immigrant's population faces a multitude of challenges in the process of integrating into the American life. On the other hand, the level of complexity of the challenge in integrating the way of life that many immigrants are likely to face is tied to their personal goals and aspirations. In other words, the higher their goals and aspirations are, the more complex and challenging it would be for the process of integration. Conversely, the average goals and aspirations involve a less complex and challenging process of integration.

Areas of challenges include, but are not limited to, employment, language, and interpersonal communication skill, awareness of social norms, education level, legal status, federal laws, and religion. Personal integration can be an asset within the immigrant population. In the United States, for example, in search of a better life and a variety of personal reasons, people face the challenge to move across the country; consequently, they face the need to integrate in the way of life, particularly to their new city or state. Immigrants who can successfully integrate in a new and unfamiliar environment are prone to easily relocate. They are also likely to get well-paying jobs. Immigrants who have average integration skills are often reluctant to relocate, and when they do, they might not see a significant change in their social life.

Why do you go away? So that you can come back. So that you can see the place you came from with new eyes and extra colors. And the people there see you differently, too. Coming back to where you started is not the same as never leaving.

—Terry Pratchett, *A Hat Full of Sky*

Culture is the whole complex of distinctive spiritual, material, intellectual and emotional features that characterizes a society or a group.

—U.N., World Commission on Culture and Development

12

TAPPING INTO YOUR CULTURAL HERITAGE

K NOWING YOUR ROOTS AND STAYING CONNECTED TO WHERE YOU COME from is a vital ingredient to shape your future and forge your identity, regardless of your walk of life. If there were someone from whom many people could learn about the importance of our individual cultural heritage, that person would be Barack H. Obama, the 44th and first African–American U.S. president ever, whose father came from Kenya, Africa and whose mother was from Kansas, in the United States of America.

MASTERING YOUR SENSE OF SELF

I N HIS JOURNEY OF DEVELOPING A STRONG SENSE OF SELF, PRESIDENT OBAMA had visited his father's homeland three times during important moments of his personal and professional life, before getting elected as President. He also went back after becoming a two-term U.S. president, the maximum length of time allowed by the Constitution. Obama visited his father's grave and his grandmother's house, to obtain the family's blessing, before taking on important matters in his life. Obama's election to the White House should encourage people across culture to rekindle their cultural heritage. Obama's successful and remarkable life's story should also inspire many people in the African American community. Many born African Americans are in search of their own identity, including cultural heritage. Some of them underestimate the importance of reconnecting with Africa. Some of them might grow into a better self after learning a little more about their cultural heritage. Forever, it is recorded in the conscious of mankind that Africa had a man whose son became the first black person ever elected to the office of U.S. president, although some Africa countries willingly participated in slavery. As Obama understood history and the power of cultural heritage to reach peak level over the course of his life, you too can tap into the life, blessing, and power that come with your individual cultural heritage.

Obama, who was named after his father (Barack Obama, Sr., former finance minister in Kenya), first visited his father's homeland between 1987 and 1988, before attending the Harvard School of Law. In that first visit, he was welcomed by his half-sister Auma, who chauffeured him around the country in a beat-up Volkswagen Beetle. He was on a mission for becoming the best of him through self-discovery. He had the opportunity to meet his paternal grandmother and had visited his father's tomb. Obama's first trip was not simply a causal visit to his father's homeland, but a way to develop a healthy sense of self, at the dawn of his academic journey in one of the Ivy League schools in the United States.

In the spring of 1990, two years after he had visited his father's homeland, Obama made history at the national level when he was elected the first African–American president of the Harvard Law Review, the highest student role at the Harvard School of Law. His first trip to Africa had a positive effect of his sense of self and identity. Several schoolmates and professors were not only struck by the ease with which he navigated complex subjects, but also by how he was settled with his sense of self.

The second trip occurred in 1992. This time he went with Michelle Obama, his fiancée at the time. They got married after that trip. Barack jokingly highlighted that the purpose of that trip was to get his grandmother's approval, which, in fact, is the custom in most African countries: to seek the family's blessing prior to a significant event like getting married. The couple's sense of cultural heritage may have also influenced their decision to have Michelle's mom stay with them even before Obama was elected President f the U.S. Next, his third visit to Kenya happened in 2006, as a senator, less than two years before he launched his presidential campaign for the office of president, on a Saturday, February 10, 2007, in Springfield, Illinois. During that trip, Obama visited, again, his father's grave and his grandmother's tin-roof house, certainly to obtain the family's blessing, before another challenge for a brighter life. In November 2008, Obama was elected the 44th U.S. president, to the amazement of many people, supporters and opponents, alike.

REFLECTING ON MEANINGFUL "CHAPTERS"

MAKING SENSE OF YOUR BIGGER LIFE STORY GOES BEYOND adulthood. It is including childhood years. some of those memories are pleasant. Other are not. Unpleasant memories can be painful to revisit. Making the attempt to reflect on it can be a way to heal from those unpleasant episodes. They are likely to prevent you from having a healthy sense of self. You should carefully go back to them in order to break free from them. You might also be able to have a fresh perspective from those painful moments in your life. Your personal story is in part connected to places you lived. By revisiting or reflecting on places where you resided for a significant period, you might be able to appreciate various aspects of your life such as achievement, life's transformations, as well as environment's changes and transformations.

You can forge the sense of self by reflecting on memories such as childhood neighborhood. Childhood memories can be pleasant and painful, but usually revitalizing and rejuvenating. Taking a time to revisit the physical place of your childhood can have a tremendous effect on your sense of identity. Your childhood place is like your place of birth, your "crib," the place that made room for you when you came to earth. It is one thing to be reminiscent of the community in which you grew up, including best memories, and it is another thing to reach out to some people you have known while growing up, including taking a trip to the places you enjoyed during your childhood and adolescence. Visiting some of those places or talking to some of the people you have known in your youth can have favorable effect on your individuality.

Your personality is made up of who you are (the nature of your character) and what you are (the nature of your being). For example, if you know yourself to be goal-driven, you might be an achiever (the nature of your character), which is one aspect of who you are. If you know yourself to be caring, it is the nature of your being. In the United States, saying "Let me be me" means telling people to let you be what or who you are.

As you grow older, your experience in life has significant effect on your personality. Some of those experiences can enhance your personality, while others can cause you to drift away from what you like about yourself.

Most people suggest experiencing a unique impression when revisiting home countries. They also stress on the distinctive feeling they get when meeting people who were part of their childhood memories. It is said that it takes a village to raise a child. Therefore, you might need to consider revisiting places and people you have come to know in order to strengthen your identity and get settle with your sense of self.

Your childhood neighborhood is your village. Your village can be a neighborhood where you grew up, or literately a country area. Taking the time to visit it is as finding your sense of self and identity, in a natural way.

You may not be in a position to visit your homeland at this time; however, you should not underestimate the valuable effect of reflecting on your cultural heritage, including various stages of your human development and growth. After all, it is said there is a child in the heart of every adult.

CLASSIC FRENCH POETRY

ALHOUGH REMINISCING CHILDHOOD EXPERIENCES IS A PERSONAL STORY, Victor Hugo (1802-1885), a poet, novelist, and one of the greatest French writers, has well described how people cherish childhood's memories, through poetry: "Lorsque L'Enfant Paraît (When the Child Appears)." The French version has been reduced in this material. The entire poem is included in English version.

Lorsque L'Enfant Paraît
by Victor Hugo

Lorsque l'enfant paraît, le cercle de famille
Applaudit à grands cris.
Son doux regard qui brille
Fait briller tous les yeux,
Et les plus tristes fronts, les plus souillés peut-être,
Se dérident soudain à voir l'enfant paraître,
Innocent et joyeux ...
Quand l'enfant vient, la joie arrive et nous éclaire.
On rit, on se récrie, on l'appelle, et sa mère
Tremble à le voir marcher...

L'enfant paraît, adieu le ciel et la patrie
Et les poètes saints ! la grave causerie
S'arrête en souriant ...

Enfant, vous êtes l'aube et mon âme est la plaine
Qui des plus douces fleurs embaume son haleine
Quand vous la respirez ...

Mon âme est la forêt dont les sombres ramures
S'emplissent pour vous seul de suaves murmures
Et de rayons dorés !
Car vos beaux yeux sont pleins de douceurs infinies,
Car vos petites mains, joyeuses et bénies,
N'ont point mal fait encor ...

Sans le comprendre encor, vous regardez le monde.
Double virginité ! corps où rien n'est immonde,
Âme où rien n'est impur !
Il est si beau, l'enfant, avec son doux sourire,
Sa douce bonne foi, sa voix qui veut tout dire,
Ses pleurs vite apaisés,
Laissant errer sa vue étonnée et ravie,
Offrant de toutes parts sa jeune âme à la vie
Et sa bouche aux baisers!
Seigneur! préservez-moi, préservez ceux que j'aime,
Frères, parents, amis, et mes ennemis même
Dans le mal triomphants,
De jamais voir, Seigneur ! l'été sans fleurs vermeilles,

La cage sans oiseaux, la ruche sans abeilles,
La maison sans enfants!

The following translation by Frankie Kemp has been chosen for this book, as it represents the apparently profound significance of belonging to a community.

When the Child Appears
(Originally written in French, "Lorsque L'Enfant Paraît,"

When the child appears, the family circle
applauds with great voices. His sweet face
which shines, makes all eyes shine,
and the saddest faces, the dirtiest,
lose their frowns suddenly seeing the child appearing,
innocent and joyous. The chairs come together,
When the child comes in,
joy arrives, and we light up.
We laugh, we cry out, we call him,
and his mother trembles
to see him walk.

Child, you are the dawn, and my soul is the field
Where the sweetest flowers give off their fragrance
as you breathe.
My soul is the forest whose sad branches
come forth at your sweet murmurs
and golden rays.
Because your beautiful eyes are pure and infinitely sweet,
Because your little happy and blessed hands
have never done evil--
Never has your innocence been touched by mire.
Sacred head!
Blond-haired child!
Beautiful angel—
A golden halo.
You are among us the dove of our ark.
Your tender and pure feet are ageless
where they walk.
Your wings are azure.
You look at the world untainted.
Twice innocent—body and soul
free from all impurities.

He is beautiful, this child, with his sweet smile.
His sweet, good faith, his voice that
appeases all our tears.
May his gaze wander to us
and astonish and rend us,
offering all of his young soul
to life
and his sweet mouth to kisses.

Lord God, save me! Save all those I love!
Brothers, family, friends,
and even my enemies
from evil's triumph.
And never let us see, Lord,
summer without
rosy flowers,
empty birdcages,
hives without bees,
or a house without children.

ACKNOWLEDGEMENTS

FIRST, I would like to thank Al Sabado, the editor of this material.

I also would like to thank those who have kindly contributed to the publication of this book: Myla Ervin, Tammy Taylor, Dr. Dave Streeter, and Georgette Koty, PhD.

Many people have directly and indirectly supportive or inspiring to me. I also want to acknowledge some of them: Emmanuel Djokou, Jerome Kameni, Emilie Bouda, Dauphine Claire Mefo, Adelaide Sambou, Sylverine Yemdo, Dieudonné Tiodi, and Marceline Nguemani.

My heartfelt appreciation goes to Sylvie Y. Tchana-Wetie, Dieudonné Mandoukou, Mélanie and Alain Moundaga, Silvio Etame, and lastly, but not the least Béatrice Ngassa, and Béatrice Matsanga,

THE FIRST BOOK

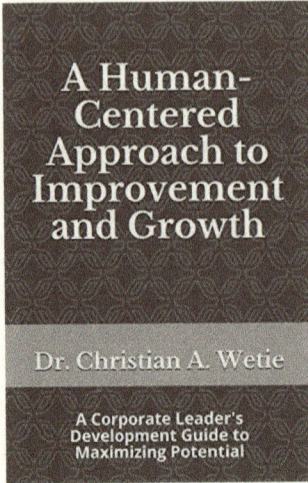

A Human-Centered Approach to Improvement and Growth

Dr. Christian A. Wetie

A Corporate Leader's Development Guide to Maximizing Potential

Many organizations in the helping profession focus on professional skills and abilities, while almost leaving out the importance of competencies related to growth and general knowledge.

Consequently, organizations in the service industry, for instance, are prone to experience high turnover rate, poor performance, and job burnout, including emotional exhaustion. This book offers a practical model to align organizational and individual improvement and growth.

It includes a model for professional and personal development, as well as individual growth.

This book is primarily intended for working professionals, managers, coaches, and trainers, as well as college students. It can be used for corporate training intervention, individual growth, professional development, and coaching.

The goal of this book is to help organizations and people maximize their potentials through a human-centered approach. It offers a unique way to improve and grow from inside out, using day-to-day concepts and principles. Now available at Amazon.com.

THE AUTHOR

D R. CHRISTIAN A. WETIE IS A LEADERSHIP MAVEN, TRAINER, COACH, and Organization Change agent. He is also the author of A *Human-Centered Approach to Improvement and Growth*. He is dedicated in inspiring people and organization to maximize their full potential. He holds a doctorate in management in global leadership, a master's in business administration in human resources management, a bachelor's degree in computer network, and has formal professional training in talent development. Dr. Christian is a member of the Council of Counseling Psychology Training Programs. During his free hours, he enjoys reading, writing, visiting touristic places, and spending quality time with family and friends.

BIBLIOGRAPHY

Ae Won Hwang, & Seo Young Kim. (2015). Differences in buying behavior of self-lovers according to the form of self-love. *Social Behavior & Personality: An International Journal, 43*(6), 993–1008. doi: 10.2224/sbp.2015.43.6.993

Align Today. (n.d.). Is our pace of life getting faster [Blog post]. Retrieved from http://blog.aligntoday.com/is-our-pace-of-life-getting-faster

Andersen, M. L., Logio, K. A., & Taylor, H. F. (2015). *Understanding society, an introductory reader.* Boston, MA: Cengage Learning.

Andrews, M. (2016). The existential crisis. *Behavioral Development Bulletin, 21*(1), 104–109. doi: 10.1037/bdb0 000014

Aronson, P. (2017, February). Contradictions in the American dream: High educational aspirations and perceptions of deteriorating institutional support. *International Journal of Psychology, 52*(1), 49–57. doi: 10.1002/ijop.12396

Bain, P., Vaes, J., Kashima, Y., Haslam, N., & Guan, Y. (2011, August 26). Folk conceptions of humanness beliefs about distinctive and core human characteristics in Australia, Italy, and China. *Journal of Cross-Cultural Psychology, 43*(1), 53–58.

Bransen, J. (2015, April). *Ethical Theory & Moral Practice, 18*(2), 309–321. doi: 10.1007/s10677-015-9578-4

Brown, B. (2011). The power of vulnerability. TEDx. Retrieved from https://www.ted.com /talks /brene _brown _on _vulnerability

Butterfield, F. (1990). First black elected to head Harvard's law review. *Special to the New York Times*. Archives, p. 00020. Retrieved from https://www.nytimes.com/1990/02/06/us /first-black-elected-to-head-harvard-s-law-review.html

Carroll, L. (n.d.). Quotable quote from "Alice in Wonderland." Good Reads website. Retrieved from https://www.goodreads.com /quotes /225938 -would-you-tell-me-please-which-way-i-ought-to

Ceyhan, A. A., & Ceyhan, E. (2011). Investigation of university students' self-acceptance and learned resourcefulness: A longitudinal study of higher education. *The International Journal of Higher Education and Educational Planning*, 61(6), 649–661.

Chuan H., Ameer, K., Jiao, H., & Kurunathan, R. (2017, April 11). Disinhibition of negative true self for identity reconstructions in cyberspace: Advancing self-discrepancy theory for virtual setting. *PLoS ONE, 12*(4), 1–19. doi: 10.1371 /journal. pone.0175623

Cole, K. (2002). *The complete idiot's guide to clear communication*. Indianapolis, IN: Alpha Books.

Connor, P., & López, G. (2016, May 18). 5 facts about the U.S. rank in worldwide migration. *Factank News in the* Numbers. Pew Research Center website. Retrieved from http://www.pewresearch.org/fact-tank/2016/05/18/5-facts-about-the-u-s-rank-in-worldwide-migration

Copeland, M. E. (2011). *Wellness recovery action plan*. Dummerston, VT: Peach Press.

Dixon L. C. (2018). The stunning transformation of Meghan Markle https://www.thelist.com/67686/stunning-transformati on-Meghan-Markle/

Fenby, J. (2010, June). The man who said "Non." *History Today*, 60(6), 35–41.

Finnegan, C. (2015, July 24). Barack Obama's trips to Kenya: Then vs. now. *ABC News*. Retrieved from http://abcnews.go.com /Politics barack –obamas -trips-kenya-now/story?id=3265 0996

First People. (n.d.). Two wolves. Native American legends. Retrieved from http://www.firstpeople.us/FP-Html -Legends/ Two Wolves-Cherokee.html

Guardo, C. J., & Bohan, J. B. (1971, December). Development of a sense of self-identity in children. *Child Development*, 42(6), 1909–1921.

Hall, T. (2015, September 16). 3 ways to develop personal authority [Web post]. Retrieved from http://drtoddhall.com /3-ways-to-develop-personal-authority

Harvard Law Today. (2008, November 1). Alumni focus: Obama first made history at HLS [Web post]. Retrieved from https://today.law.harvard.edu/obama-first-made-history-at-hls/

Hill, P. C., & Sandage, S. J. (2016, June). The promising but challenging case of humility as a positive psychology virtue. *Journal of Moral Education*, 45(2), 132–146. doi: 10.1080 /03057240.2016.1174675

Hofstede, G., Hofstede G. J., & Minkov, M. (2010). *Cultures and organizations: Software of the mind*. New York, NY: McGraw Hill.

Holden, S. (2006, October 20). Kool-aid, craziness and Utopian yearning. *New York Times*. Retrieved from http://www .nytimes.com /2006/10/20/movies/20temp.html

Hoover Institution. (2015a). *Uncommon knowledge with Peter Robinson: The secretary of state and her instructor play well together* [YouTube video]. Available from https://www .youtube.com/watch?v=1Q0tDKtYojI

Hoover Institution. (2015b). *Uncommon knowledge with Peter Robinson: The secretary of state, the instructor, and the piano* [YouTube video]. Available from https://www .youtube.com/watch?v=iwGlrVLcqUQ

Hugo, V. (n.d.). *Lorsque l'enfant paraît.* Retrieved from http://poesie.webnet.fr/lesgrandsclassiques/poemes /victor _hugo /lorsque_l_enfant_parait.html. English translation by Frankie Kemp, When the Child Appears, 2015. Retrieved from https://www.faithwriters.com /critique -circle-details .php?id=13138

Hunt, J. G. (1996). *Leadership. A new synthesis.* Newbury Park, CA: SAGE.

Kennedy Center. (2017). *Yo-Yo Ma and Condoleezza Rice perform Schumann's "Fantasiestücke, Op, 73"* [YouTube video]. Available from https://www.youtube.com /watch ?v=T4C-VuqubFM

Kets de Vries, M. F. R. (2003). *Leaders, fools, and impostors.* Lincoln, NE: iUniverse, Inc.

King, S. N., & Lee, R. J. (2001). *Discovering the leader in you. A guide to realizing your personal leadership potential.* San Francisco, CA: Jossey-Bass.

Kistner, J., David, C., & Repper, K. (2007, February). Self-enhancement of peer acceptance: Implications for children's self-worth and interpersonal functioning. *Social Development, 16*(1), 24–44.

Laing, A., & Weston, P. (2015, July 24). Barack Obama in Kenya: How this trip compares to his 1987 visit. *The Telegraph.* Retrieved from https://www.telegraph.co.uk /news /worldnews/africaandindianocean/kenya/11761025/Barac k- Obama -in -Kenya -how-this-trip -compares-to-his-1987-visit.html

Lamanna, F., Lenormand, M., Salas-Olmedo, M. H., Romanillos, G., Gonçalves, B., & Ramasco, J. J. (2018, March 14). Immigrant community integration in world cities. *PLoS ONE, 13*(3), 1–19. doi: 10.1371/journal.pone.0191612

Leasca, S. (2017, October 30). Here's the very scary amount of money Americans spend on Halloween. *Forbes:* Investing. Retrieved from https://www.forbes.com/sites/sleasca/2017/10/30/halloween-spending-halloween-candy

Li, J. (2016). Humility in learning: A Confucian perspective. *Journal of Moral Education, 45*(2), 147–165.

Lipsyte, R. (2016, June 4). Muhammad Ali dies at 74: Titan of boxing and the 20th century. *The New York Times.* Retrieved from https://www.nytimes.com /2016 /06 /04/ sports /muhammad-ali-dies.html

MacKenzie, M. B., & Kocovski, N. L. (2010). Self-reported acceptance of social anxiety symptoms: Development and validation of the social anxiety-acceptance and action questionnaire. *International Journal of Behavioral Consultation and Therapy, 6*(3), 214–232.

Mansfield, H. (n.d.). Niccolò Machiavelli: Italian statesman and writer. *Encyclopaedia Britannica.* Retrieved from https: //www.britannica.com /biography /Niccolo-Machiavelli

Matei, R. M. (2017, July–December). The false self and the construction of identity in the psychoanalytic process. *Romanian Journal of Psychoanalysis / Revue Roumain de Psychanalyse, 10*(2), 189–198. doi: 10.26336/rjp.2017-1002-11

McGrath, M. (2016, January 6). 63% of Americans don't have enough savings to cover a $500 emergency. *Forbes: Investing.* Retrieved from https://www.forbes.com/sites /maggiemcgrath/2016/01 /06/ 63-of-americans-dont-have-enough-savings-to- cover-a- 500- emergency /#50122c684 e0d

Moseley, A. (2008). *A to Z of philosophy.* New York, NY: Continuum International Publishing Group.

Myers, S. (2016, June). Myers-Briggs typology and Jungian individuation. *Journal of Analytical Psychology, 61*(3), 289–308. doi: 10.1111/1468-5922.12233

Myers & Briggs Foundation. (n.d.). Objectives and mission. Retrieved from http://www.myersbriggs.org /myers-and-briggs-foundation/objectives-and-mission

Nevid, J. S. (2003). *Psychology concepts and applications.* San Diego, CA: Charles Hartford.

Ofole, N. M. (2017). Self-acceptance of students repeating classes in Ibadan Metropolis: Relationship with parents' sense of competence, locus of control and quality of parents-child relationship. *IFE PsychologIA, 25*(2), 133–150.

Orbe, M. P., & Bruess, J. C. (2005). *Contemporary issues in interpersonal communication.* Los Angeles, CA: Roxbury Publishing Company.

Pavulraj, M. S. J. (2015, October). Jñana yoga in the Bhagavad Gita: The path for self-realization. *Asia Journal of Theology, 29*(2), 195–226.

Pettitt, G. A. (1970). *Prisoners of culture.* New York, NY: Charles Scribner's Sons.

Quizlet. (n.d.). Crisis and crisis intervention [Flash cards]. Retrieved from https://quizlet.com/5451731/crisis-and-crisis-intervention-flash-cards

Rodriguez, M. (2018, February 1). The kings of big spring: God, oil, and one family's search for the American dream. *Library Journal, 143*(2), 107–108.

Roizen, M. F., Oz, M. C., & Rome, E. (2011). *You, the owner's manual for teens: A guide to a healthy body and happy life.* New York, NY: Free Press.

Society for Human Resource Management. (SHRM, 2016). *Employee job satisfaction and engagement: Revitalizing a changing workforce*. A research report by the SHRM. Retrieved from https://www.shrm.org/hr-today/trends-and-forecasting / research - and - surveys /Documents/2016-Employee-Job-Satisfaction-and-Engagement-Report.pdf

Strayer University. (2003). *Principles of organizational behavior* (12th ed.). Upper Saddle River, NJ: Prentice Hall.

Surbhi S. (2016, March 21). Difference between personality and character [Web post]. Key Differences website. Retrieved from https://keydifferences.com /difference -between-personality-and-character.html

Tucker, A. R. (2011). An assessment of the Myers Briggs Type Indicator from a practical theological perspective, *Acta Theologica, 31*(2), 295–314.

United States Census Bureau. (2017, January 10). National African–American history month: February 2017. *Facts for Features*. Retrieved from https://www.census.gov /newsroom/facts-for-features/2017/cb17-ff01.html

United States Court of Appeals. (1971, June 28). Cassius Marsellus CLAY, Jr. also known as Muhammad Ali, Petitioner, v. United States. No. 783. Retrieved from the Cornell Law School website, https://www.law.cornell.edu/supreme court/text/403/698

Varga, S. (2011, February). Self-realization and owing to others: An indirect constraint? *International Journal of Philosophical Studies, 19*(1), 75–86. doi: 10.1080/09672559.2011.539362

Virtues for Life. (n.d.). Two Wolves. Retrieved from http://www.virtuesforlife.com/two-wolves

Wetie, C. A. (2018). *A human-centered approach to improvement and growth*. Greensboro, NC: Christian A. Wetie.

Wilking, S., & Effron, L. (2014, February 17). Snake-handling Pentecostal pastor dies from snake bite. *ABC News*. Retrieved from http://abcnews.go.com/US/snake-handling-pentecostal-pastor-dies-snake-bite/story?id=22551754

Williamson, M. (n.d.). Home page. Retrieved from https://marianne.com/

Ye Hee Lee, M. (2015, July 7). Yes, U.S. locks people up at a higher rate than any other country. *The Washington Post*. Retrieved from https://www.washingtonpost.com /news/fact-checker /wp /2015/07/07/yes-u-s-locks-people-up-at-a-higher-rate -than-any-other -country/?utm_term= .a23e129a6702

Young, A. (2017, December 13). Deer leap to their deaths, stunning motorists. From *USA Today*, reposted on *MSN News*. Retrieved from https://www.msn.com/en-us/news/us/deer-leap-to-their-deaths-stunning-motorists/ar-BBGFGbi?li=BB nb7Kz

Zeuschner B. R. (2001). *Classical ethics: East and west*. New York, NY: McGraw-Hill Companies.

INDEX

A

actual self, 13, 26, 27
admiration, 6, 91, 92
adult crime, xi
adulthood, xiii, xiv, 22, 62, 63, 75, 84
adventurer, 127, 128, 131, 137, 143
Africa, 43, 96, 109, 134, 136, 152, 161, 162, 163
African American, 113, 161, 163
American dream, xvii, xviii, xix, 174, 181
anthropology, xi
anxiety, 20, 73, 88
aspirations, xv, xxi, 6, 20, 23, 27, 35, 37, 40, 43, 76, 94, 103, 129, 130, 140, 143, 148, 149, 150, 151, 153, 154, 156, 174

B

Barack Obama, xvi, 110, 121, 162, 176, 178
best self, 98, 130, 141
Bill Gates, 121
biological parent, 25
black, 113, 155, 162, 176
blue-collar crime, xv
brain, 20, 23, 24, 25, 149
Brené Brown, 129

C

Cat, 7, 8
Charles de Gaulle, 95, 97
childhood, xii, xiii, xiv, 6, 22, 29, 33, 43, 62, 63, 65, 75, 117, 118, 119, 120, 154, 164, 165
China, 102, 152, 174
clear identity, xxi, 8, 27, 62, 64
competencies
human, 173
comprehensive concept, 13
Condoleezza Rice, 112
confused, 8, 25, 57, 73, 77
conscience, 113
crime, xv
cultural heritage, 141, 142, 143, 155, 161, 162, 165, See heritage

D

David Frost, 59, 147, 149
depression, 25, 74
depressive disorder, 73
development
satisfied life, 173
deviant, xi, 28, 75
discrimination, xix, 28
gender, xi
racial, xi

divine intervention, 106
dysfunctional home, 29

E

Erik Erikson, 5, 62
everyday challenges
    everyday challenges, xx
existential crisis, 20, 22
extroverted, 52, 103, 104

F

false humility, 108, 110, *See*
    humility
false self, 71, *See self*
family heritage, 76, *See*
    heritage
financial freedom, xx
France, 95, 96, 102, 107
freedom, xvii
French, 95, 97, 165
Frost/Nixon, 147
full potential, *173*

G

gaining insights, 33
goals, 14, 23, 27, 33, 37, 43,
    54, 61, 62, 63, 76, 84, 90,
    135, 136, 137, 140, 143,
    149, 150, 153, 156
Google search, 13
groupthink, 141, 142

H

Halloween, 71, 72, 180

happiness, xvii, xviii, 6, 10,
    11, 27, 98, 147, *See*
    lasting happiness
Harvard Law Review, 121,
    163
heart, 23, 26, 136, 149, 150,
    165
heritage, 76, 155, 156, 161,
    164
    cultural, 141
    family, 76
    personal, 155
homeland, 131, 132, 161,
    162, 165
human civilization, x, 106
humility, 94, 101, 104, 106,
    108, 109, 110, 111, 112,
    114, 119, 177
    false, 108
    is not, 111
    true, 111

I

identity, 5, xii, xvi, xviii, 3, 5,
    6, 7, 8, 10, 11, 13, 14, 15,
    21, 22, 25, 26, 27, 28, 29,
    30, 33, 37, 56, 57, 62, 64,
    70, 72, 75, 76, 77, 90, 106,
    114, 127, 133, 134, 135,
    136, 140, 141, 155, 161,
    162, 164, 165, 176, 177,
    180
    clear, 8
    personal, 27
    rich, xii, 8
identity clarity, 22, 77

identity crisis, 21, 22, 26, 28,
   29, 30, 63, 70, 72
immigrants, xviii, xix, xx, 130,
   131, 134, 135, 136, 139,
   141, 153, 155, 156
immigration, 125
impostor syndrome, 70, 72
incarceration, xii, xx
individual crisis, 26
individualistic society, xx, 54
ingenuity, 136
inside out, xxi, 36, 38, 40, 77,
   85, 129, 130, 150
introverted, 52, 103, 104
Isabel Briggs Myers, 49, 51,
   115
Iyanla Vanzant, 98

K

Katharine Cook, 51
Kenya, 161, 162, 163, 176,
   178

L

Las Vegas, 132
lasting happiness, xxi, 10
lemonade, 29
lemons, 29
Lewis Carrol, 7
life satisfaction, xx, 11, 136,
   147
lion, 13, 96
lower-order, 6

M

Machiavellianism, 51, 52,
   53
magnetic north, 36, 37
Manhattan, 132
Mary E. Copeland, 19
maturation, x, xi, xiii, 22, 23,
   24, 25, 28
maturational crisis, 22, 24,
   25, 26
mental illness, xx
Michelle Obama, 163
missionary, 130, 141
Muhammad Ali, 113

N

narcissism, 51, 90, 91
Natural Identity, 5
Nelson Mandela, 121
neuron
   neuronal, neurons, 24
Nixon, 147, 148
nonjudgmental, 84, 86, 89,
   96
non-U.S. born American,
   151
non-U.S. born citizens, xviii,
   xix, 151
North Korea, 110

O

old age, xii, xiii
ought self, 26, 27
overcoming, xix, xx, 34, 106,
   130

adversities, 34
conflict, 153
discrimination, xix
everyday challenges, xx
language barrier, xix
pain and affliction, 106
racial prejudice, xix
typical challenges, xix

P

pathological behavior, xx
Patricia Wald, 121
perfectionism, 83, 88, 89,
    95, 96
personal accountability, ix,
    93
personal authority, 109,
    155, 177
personal heritage, 155, See
    heritage
personal identity, 7, 25, 56,
    62, 72, See identity
personal integration, 156
personality masks, 71, 73
personality type, 53, 104
philosophy, 128
physical appearance, xxi
Plato, 108
preferences, 8, 55, 64, 94,
    115, 117, 119, 120, 121,
    149
proactive personality, 51,
    55
professional and
    organizational attributes,
    52
pruning, 22, 23, 24, 25

psychiatry, 69, 71
psychology, 23, 51, 56, 63,
    64, 65, 69, 71, 74, 101,
    102, 111, 164, 177
pure perfectionism, 83, 84

Q

Queen Elizabeth, 110

R

racial prejudice, xix, See
    discrimination,
    overcoming
rich identity, xii, xxii, 9, 29,
    37, 83, 88
risk-taking, 51, 53

S

satisfaction, 6, 10, 11, 12,
    66, 181, See life
    satisfaction
self, 4, ix, x, xv, xvii, xviii, xix,
    xx, xxii, 5, 6, 7, 8, 9, 10, 12,
    13, 14, 15, 16, 20, 21, 26,
    27, 30, 33, 34, 37, 38, 40,
    45, 51, 55, 61, 63, 64, 65,
    69, 70, 71, 72, 73, 74, 75,
    76, 83, 86, 87, 88, 89, 90,
    91, 92, 93, 94, 96, 97, 98,
    102, 103, 106, 109, 110,
    111, 114, 119, 120, 127,
    129, 130, 135, 137, 139,
    141, 143, 147, 150, 152,
    162, 165, 174, 176, 177,
    178, 180, 181

ideal, 26
ought, 26
true, x, 71
self-acceptance, xxii, 83,
    86, 88, 89, 90
self-actualization, x, 6, 73,
    103, 130
self-admiration, 6, 91
self-attainment, 103
self-care, 74, 93, 97, 137
self-concept, 5, 14, 70
self-confidence, 15, 63, 64,
    87, 88, 109, 114
self-discovery, 34, 93, 139,
    143, 162
self-empowerment, 111
self-esteem, 5, 13, 74, 91,
    119, 120
self-examination, 34
self-identity, 7, x, xviii, xx, 5,
    6, 7, 8, 9, 10, 12, 13, 15,
    16, 20, 27, 33, 38, 55, 61,
    62, 63, 65, 69, 72, 74, 76,
    103, 127, 129, 130, 131,
    135, 143, 147
self-image, 5, 13, 41, 45, 93
self-inflicted, 37, 93
self-realization, 7, 9, 16, 73,
    130, 143, 181
self-sabotage, 132
self-value, 86
self-worth, 5, 10, 14, 15, 65,
    91, 119, 120, 178
serenity, 84, 89, 94, 95, 96
setbacks, 33, 34, 40, 73, 92,
    95, 96
settlers, 130, 131
SHRM, 11, 181

social acceptance, 87
social anxiety, 87
social evaluation, 87
social learning, x, 92, 151
sociology, xi, 69, 74, 141
Socrates, 107
soul-searching, 34, 139
South Korea, 109
South Side of Chicago, 121
spy, xx, 130
Steve Jobs, 43, 101, 121
stuck, xi, 8, 57, 63, 73
sub-Sahara Africa, 109

T

theological, x, 182
tourism, 134, 135
tourist syndrome, 135
true humility, 111, See
    humility
true north, 34, 35, 36, 37, 41
true self, ix, xix, 9, 37, 40, 71,
    73, 141, 150, See self

U

U.S. born citizens, xviii, xix,
    xx, 151
U.S. population, xii, xvii, xviii,
    xx, 151
U.S. President, 53, 121, 161,
    162, 163
unapologetic, 112, 114
understanding crises, 19

V

values, 33, 35, 40, 43, 62,
88, 103, 108, 109, 117,
120, 121, 129, 149, 153
values preferences, 120
voice, 99, 114, 120, 121, 130

vulnerability, 129, 132, 174

W

Washington, D.C., 132
white-collar crimes, xv

www.ingramcontent.com/pod-product-compliance
Lightning Source LLC
Chambersburg PA
CBHW031253090426
42742CB00007B/436

* 9 780692 133255 *